BEYOND THE BASICS: ADVANCED STRATEGIES FOR INDIE AUTHOR SUCCESS

Multi-Award-Winning-Author
B Alan Bourgeois

B Alan Bourgeois

Beyond the Basics: Advanced Strategies for Indie Author Success

© B Alan Bourgeois 2025

All rights reserved. No part of this publication may be reproduced, stored in a retrieval system, or transmitted in any form or by any means, electronic, mechanical, photocopying, recording, or otherwise, without the prior written permission of the publisher.

The information and opinions expressed in this book are believed to be accurate and reliable, but no responsibility or liability is assumed by the publisher for any errors, omissions, or any damages caused by the use of these products, procedures, or methods presented herein.

The book is sold and distributed on an "as is" basis without warranties of any kind, either expressed or implied, including but not limited to warranties of merchantability or fitness for a particular purpose. The purchaser or reader of this book assumes complete responsibility for the use of these materials and information.

Any legal disputes arising from the use of this book shall be governed by the laws of the jurisdiction where the book was purchased, without regard to its conflict of law provisions, and shall be resolved exclusively in the courts of that jurisdiction.

ISBN: 979-8-3484-5289-6

Publisher: Bourgeois Media & Consulting (BourgeoisMedia.com)

Beyond the Basics

B ALAN BOUERGEOIS

50

STORYTELLING
LITERACY & HERITAGE

Thank you for purchasing this limited edition book, offered in celebration of the author's 50-year milestone. Proceeds from your purchase support the Texas Authors Institute of History, a museum founded by the author in 2015, dedicated to preserving the legacy of Texas authors.

https://TexasAuthors.Institute

B Alan Bourgeois

Dear Fellow Authors,

I'm delighted to introduce this book—and every guide in this series—as a short, easy-to-read resource designed to help you succeed in your writing journey. As writers, our true passion lies in creating stories, and I understand that delving into the business side of publishing might not be where we wish to spend most of our time.

That's why I've made a conscious effort to keep things simple and straightforward, focusing on practical advice without unnecessary fluff. You'll find that some concepts overlap between books, and that's intentional—to reinforce key ideas and ensure that whichever guide you pick up, you're equipped with valuable tools to enhance your success.

I genuinely hope you find these guides enjoyable and helpful. Your feedback means the world to me, and I look forward to hearing about your experiences and triumphs.

Happy writing, and here's to your continued success!

Beyond the Basics

Introduction

Welcome to *Empowering Authors: Top Strategies for Writing Success and Career Growth.* Whether you're an aspiring writer taking your first steps or an experienced author looking to refine your craft, this guide is designed to provide you with practical, proven strategies to navigate today's ever-evolving publishing landscape.

In a world that's more connected than ever, the opportunities to share your work have expanded exponentially. However, success in writing requires more than just creativity—it demands adaptability, strategy, and persistence. Drawing from years of experience as an author advocate and consultant, I've distilled these strategies by observing what consistently leads to success for writers across genres and publishing paths.

Each chapter in this book offers insights, actionable steps, and real-world examples of authors who have applied these strategies to achieve their goals. From establishing a sustainable writing habit to mastering the complexities of marketing, publishing, and even leveraging technology, this book equips you with the tools you need to build a fulfilling and lasting writing career.

Why These Strategies Matter
The strategies outlined in this book are not just theoretical concepts; they are practical methods that have helped authors realize their creative and professional dreams. Whether you're navigating the complexities of self-publishing, seeking a traditional book deal, or exploring new income streams beyond books, each chapter is designed to provide clarity and direction in your writing journey.

B Alan Bourgeois

From daily habits to effective marketing plans, from overcoming writer's block to embracing technology, this book covers every aspect of a writer's career development, ensuring you're prepared for the challenges and rewards that lie ahead.

What You'll Gain from This Book
By the end of this book, you'll have a comprehensive understanding of:
1. **Daily Writing Habits:** How to build and maintain a consistent writing practice that keeps you productive.
2. **Reading for Improvement:** Learning to read critically to improve your storytelling skills.
3. **Community and Feedback:** Finding and engaging with a supportive writing network to elevate your craft.
4. **Mastering Editing:** Approaching revision as an integral part of the writing process.
5. **Effective Marketing:** Creating a tailored marketing plan to reach your target audience.
6. **Building an Online Presence:** Establishing your author brand and connecting with readers digitally.
7. **Setting Realistic Goals:** Using SMART goals to stay motivated and track progress.
8. **Handling Rejection:** Transforming setbacks into opportunities for growth.
9. **Seeking Professional Help:** Understanding when and how to invest in expert assistance to elevate your work.
10. **Staying True to Your Authentic Voice:** Writing with honesty and maintaining your unique style.
11. **Time Management for Writers:** Balancing writing with life's responsibilities and maximizing productivity.
12. **Self-Publishing vs. Traditional Publishing:** Exploring the pros and cons of different publishing routes.
13. **Monetizing Your Writing Beyond Books:** Generating income through multiple writing-related opportunities.
14. **Writing Across Multiple Genres:** Navigating the challenges and benefits of multi-genre writing.

15. **Overcoming Writer's Block and Burnout:** Strategies to reignite your creativity and stay motivated.
16. **Writing for a Global Audience:** Adapting your work to resonate with readers worldwide.
17. **Leveraging AI and Technology in Writing:** Utilizing cutting-edge tools to enhance your writing and marketing efforts.

How to Use This Book

Each chapter is designed as a standalone resource, allowing you to focus on what's most relevant to your current writing needs. However, I encourage you to explore every strategy, as they interconnect to create a cohesive framework for writing success. Whether you're seeking to improve your writing discipline, navigate the publishing world, or expand your income streams, you'll find actionable advice and inspiring case studies to guide you.

Remember, every writer's journey is unique—what works for one author may not work for another. Adapt these strategies to fit your personal goals and creative process, and trust your instincts along the way. Writing is a lifelong journey of growth, and with the right mindset and tools, you can build a sustainable and rewarding career.

"Writing is not about being inspired; it's about staying committed."

Thank you for choosing *Empowering Authors: Top Strategies for Writing Success and Career Growth*. May these strategies serve as your roadmap, guiding you toward a fulfilling and impactful writing career.

Happy writing!

B Alan Bourgeois

Contents

1. Daily Writing Habits. — 9
2. Reading for Improvement — 12
3. Community and Feedback. — 18
4. Mastering Editing: — 25
5. Effective Marketing — 32
6. Building an Online Presence. — 39
7. Setting Realistic Goals — 42
8. Handling Rejection — 47
9. Seeking Professional Help. — 53
10. Staying True to Your Authentic Voice — 59
11. Time Management for Writers. — 65
12. Self-Publishing vs. Traditional Publishing — 72
13. Monetizing Your Writing Beyond Books — 78
14. Writing Across Multiple Genres — 85
15. Overcoming Writer's Block and Burnout — 92
16. Writing for a Global Audience — 98
17. Leveraging AI and Technology in Writing — 105

About the Author — 112
Other Books by the Author in this Series — 113

1
Write Every Day

The Power of Daily Practice
Writing every day is one of the most effective habits an author can build. It's not about creating perfection in a single sitting; it's about establishing momentum. A daily writing habit strengthens your creativity, builds discipline, and helps you maintain a connection to your work.

As Stephen King writes in *On Writing*:
"Amateurs sit and wait for inspiration, the rest of us just get up and go to work."

Even if you're only writing for 15 minutes, those daily sessions add up over time. For instance:
- Writing 200 words per day equals **73,000 words** in a year. That's a novel!
- Daily practice can also help you break through writer's block, as the act of writing itself generates ideas.

Why It Matters
Consistency is more important than inspiration. Writing daily:
- **Develops Your Voice:** Writing regularly sharpens your unique style.
- **Builds Confidence:** Small, consistent wins encourage you to tackle bigger projects.
- **Overcomes Resistance:** The hardest part of writing is starting, and a habit makes starting automatic.

Practical Tips to Build a Daily Writing Habit
1. **Set a Goal You Can Achieve:**
    - Start with a manageable daily word count (e.g., 200 words or 15 minutes).

        - Use apps like *Scrivener* or *4theWords* to track your progress.
2. **Create a Schedule and Stick to It:**
        - Find a time of day when you're least likely to be interrupted.
        - Write at the same time every day to train your brain to expect it.
3. **Eliminate Distractions:**
        - Turn off notifications on your phone or use focus apps like *Freedom* or *Forest*.
        - Set up a dedicated writing space, even if it's just a specific chair or desk corner.
4. **Use Prompts or Write Freely:**
        - Stuck on what to write? Use prompts from *Writer's Digest* or the *Writing Prompts subreddit*.
        - Freewriting (stream-of-consciousness writing) can help clear mental clutter.

Examples of Successful Daily Writers

- **Stephen King** writes 2,000 words every day, finishing by lunchtime to allow his afternoons for reading.
- **J.K. Rowling** wrote much of *Harry Potter* in cafés during short writing sessions, proving that consistency works even with a busy schedule.
- **Case Study:** Maya, a novice writer, participated in *NaNoWriMo* (National Novel Writing Month). Writing 1,667 words daily for a month helped her complete her first draft. By continuing a scaled-down version of this habit, she completed a second novel in under a year.

Reflection Questions

- When during the day do you feel most creative or focused?
- What obstacles are preventing you from writing daily, and how can you address them?

Beyond the Basics

Action Step
Commit to a **7-day writing challenge.** Each day, write for 15 minutes or aim for 200 words. Track your progress and note any patterns in your productivity or creativity.

2
Read Widely and Often

Why Reading Improves Writing
Reading isn't just a pastime for writers; it's an essential tool for mastering the craft. By exposing yourself to different voices, genres, and styles, you gain insights that can significantly improve your own writing. As author Stephen King famously said in *On Writing*,

"If you don't have time to read, you don't have the time (or the tools) to write."

Great writers are also great readers. Reading helps you understand storytelling techniques, character development, dialogue flow, and narrative structure. Moreover, it exposes you to different perspectives, allowing you to expand your creativity and strengthen your voice.

The Benefits of Reading as a Writer
1. **Expanding Your Literary Toolkit**
    - Reading widely introduces you to various writing styles, sentence structures, and storytelling techniques. By analyzing how different authors handle dialogue, description, and pacing, you can incorporate similar elements into your own writing.
    - **Example:** Ernest Hemingway's concise, punchy style contrasts with Jane Austen's elaborate, descriptive prose. Studying both can teach you how brevity and richness can serve different storytelling purposes.

Beyond the Basics

2. **Understanding Genre Conventions**
   - Every genre has its unique expectations. Reading within your genre helps you master the tropes readers expect, while reading outside your genre can inspire fresh ideas and unique cross-genre storytelling.
   - **Example:** A thriller writer reading romance might learn how to add emotional depth to their characters, making their stories more relatable.
3. **Learning from Mistakes Without Making Them**
   - Reading allows you to observe what works—and what doesn't—without having to experience trial and error yourself. Whether it's overused clichés, plot holes, or flat characters, seeing these pitfalls in other works can help you avoid them.
4. **Improving Language Skills**
   - Exposure to high-quality writing enhances your vocabulary, grammar, and sentence construction. You'll naturally absorb new words and sentence structures, which can elevate your own writing style.

How to Read Like a Writer
Reading as a writer means going beyond passive enjoyment and actively analyzing the text to extract useful lessons. Here's how to do it effectively:

1. Analyze Story Structure
- Break down the book into its key components:
  - **Beginning:** How does the author hook the reader?
  - **Middle:** What keeps the story engaging?
  - **End:** How does the resolution satisfy (or subvert) expectations?
- **Exercise:** Take one of your favorite books and outline its three-act structure. What patterns do you notice?

2. Pay Attention to Character Development
- Observe how authors introduce and evolve their characters. Are their motivations clear? Do they grow throughout the story?
- **Exercise:** Choose a character from a novel and write a one-paragraph analysis of their development from start to finish.

3. Study Dialogue and Pacing
- Good dialogue feels natural and serves a purpose. Notice how the author uses dialogue to reveal information, deepen relationships, or create tension.
- **Example:** In *The Catcher in the Rye*, J.D. Salinger's use of authentic teenage slang makes Holden Caulfield's voice memorable and relatable.

4. Examine Writing Style
- Identify the author's voice, tone, and use of literary devices (metaphors, similes, symbolism).
- **Exercise:** Try mimicking the style of different authors to better understand their approach to writing.

5. Take Notes and Reflect
- Keep a reading journal where you jot down insights, favorite quotes, and techniques you'd like to try in your writing.
- Use prompts such as:
    - What did I love about this book?
    - What would I do differently if I were writing this story?
    - How can I apply this to my current project?

Expanding Your Reading Horizons
Reading widely means stepping outside your comfort zone and exploring diverse genres, authors, and cultures. This not only enriches your perspective but also adds depth and originality to your writing.

Beyond the Basics

Genres to Explore:
1. **Fiction:** Novels, short stories, flash fiction (literary, speculative, historical, etc.).
2. **Non-Fiction:** Memoirs, self-help, history, science, philosophy.
3. **Poetry:** Reading poetry can inspire rhythm and conciseness in your prose.
4. **Plays and Screenplays:** These teach effective dialogue and visual storytelling.
5. **International Literature:** Translated works expose you to different storytelling traditions and cultures.

Action Step: Choose a book from a genre you rarely read and analyze what stands out in its storytelling style.

Case Studies: Authors Who Read Widely
Neil Gaiman – The Power of Diverse Influences
Neil Gaiman is known for drawing inspiration from mythology, comic books, and classic literature. His reading habits have contributed to his unique blend of fantasy and reality in books like *American Gods*.

Lesson: Reading a wide variety of material can inspire fresh, original ideas in your writing.

2. Chimamanda Ngozi Adichie – Embracing Cultural Perspectives
Adichie's work draws on Nigerian literature, global history, and contemporary fiction. Her diverse reading allows her to create complex, multi-layered characters and themes in novels like *Half of a Yellow Sun*.

Lesson: Diverse reading helps bring authenticity and depth to your storytelling.

3. Stephen King – Reading for Inspiration and Technique
King attributes much of his storytelling ability to his voracious

reading habit. He emphasizes how reading across different genres has influenced his writing techniques in pacing and character development.

Lesson: Read not just to enjoy, but to analyze what works and apply it to your writing.

Practical Reading Strategies for Writers
1. **Set Reading Goals:**
   - Aim to read a book a month related to your genre and another outside it.
   - Balance fiction and non-fiction to enhance your storytelling and knowledge.
2. **Use Audiobooks:**
   - Listening to audiobooks can help you analyze storytelling through narration and dialogue delivery.
3. **Join Book Clubs:**
   - Engaging in discussions with fellow readers can provide fresh insights you might not have considered.
4. **Read With Intent:**
   - Before starting a book, decide what you want to learn—dialogue, pacing, character development, etc.

Reflection Questions
- What genres have you neglected in your reading, and how might exploring them benefit your writing?
- Are there specific authors you admire? What elements of their writing style can you study and incorporate?
- How can you build a consistent reading habit into your daily routine?

Action Steps
1. Choose a book from an unfamiliar genre and read it with a focus on structure and character development.

Beyond the Basics

2. Start a reading journal to document your favorite techniques and observations.
3. Join an online reading challenge to diversify your reading list.

Reading widely and often isn't just about entertainment—it's about growth. The more you read with purpose, the more tools you'll have at your disposal as a writer. Whether it's learning how to craft gripping suspense, develop deeper characters, or create vivid worlds, the lessons are all waiting for you between the pages.

So, grab a book, open your mind, and let your reading journey fuel your writing success.

3
Finding a Writing Community

Why Community Matters for Writers

Writing is often seen as a solitary pursuit, but the truth is that no writer succeeds alone. Whether you're looking for feedback, motivation, or camaraderie, being part of a supportive writing community can significantly impact your growth and long-term success. A writing community provides encouragement, accountability, and valuable insights that help you refine your craft and stay inspired.

"Surround yourself with people who believe in your dreams, encourage your ideas, support your ambitions, and bring out the best in you." – Roy T. Bennett

A strong writing community can:
- **Provide constructive feedback** to improve your writing.
- **Offer accountability** to keep you motivated and on track.
- **Help navigate the publishing process** with shared resources and advice.
- **Combat isolation** by surrounding yourself with like-minded individuals who understand the challenges of being a writer.

The Different Types of Writing Communities

Not all writing communities are the same, and it's important to find one that aligns with your goals, personality, and writing style. Below are the various types of writing communities you can explore:

Beyond the Basics

1. Local Writing Groups
Many cities and towns have writing groups that meet regularly in libraries, bookstores, or community centers. These groups offer face-to-face interaction, fostering deep connections and trust among members.

Benefits:
- Personalized, in-depth critiques from members who know your work over time.
- Opportunities to attend local events, book signings, and workshops.
- Networking possibilities with local authors, publishers, and bookstores.

Where to Find Them:
- Local libraries or bookstores.
- Meetup.com or Facebook events.
- Writing workshops and retreats.

Case Study:
David, an aspiring thriller writer, joined a local writing group in his town. Through weekly meetings and shared critiques, he refined his manuscript and eventually found a mentor who helped him land a literary agent.

Action Step: Research writing groups in your area and attend at least one meeting to explore the fit.

2. Online Writing Communities
The internet has made it easier than ever to connect with fellow writers from around the world. Online writing communities offer flexibility and access to a wide range of perspectives, genres, and experiences.

Benefits:
- Connect with writers across different genres and backgrounds.
- Access 24/7 support and discussions.

- Participate in critique exchanges without leaving your home.

Popular Online Writing Communities:
- **Scribophile:** A critique-based platform where you can exchange feedback with fellow writers.
- **Wattpad:** A platform for sharing serialized stories and engaging with a broad audience.
- **Reddit (r/writing, r/writers):** A forum-based community for discussions and advice.
- **Critique Circle:** An online space for exchanging detailed manuscript critiques.

Example:
Indie author Maria built a large following on Wattpad by sharing short stories. The platform's supportive community helped her gain confidence and led to a traditional publishing deal.

Action Step: Join an online writing community today and start engaging in discussions or sharing your work.

3. Writing Workshops and Conferences

Attending writing workshops or conferences can provide valuable insights from industry professionals and allow you to connect with like-minded writers. Whether in-person or virtual, these events offer structured learning and networking opportunities.

Benefits:
- Learn from experienced authors, agents, and editors.
- Get personalized feedback on your work through workshop sessions.
- Discover new publishing opportunities and market trends.

Notable Conferences and Workshops:
- **Writer's Digest Conference (USA):** Offers workshops and networking with top publishing professionals.

Beyond the Basics

- **The London Book Fair (UK):** Great for networking and pitching your book to publishers.
- **NaNoWriMo (National Novel Writing Month):** An online event that fosters a supportive writing community.

Case Study:
Tim attended a writing conference where he pitched his book to an agent and received invaluable feedback that helped him secure a book deal.

Action Step: Research upcoming writing conferences or online workshops and sign up for one that aligns with your goals.

How to Find the Right Writing Community for You
Not every writing group or platform will be the right fit, and it's important to evaluate your personal writing needs when choosing a community. Consider the following:
1. **Your Writing Goals:**
    - Are you looking for publication support, casual camaraderie, or accountability?
    - Do you need critique partners, or are you seeking inspiration and encouragement?
2. **Your Genre:**
    - Some groups cater specifically to genres like romance, sci-fi, or memoir.
    - Ensure the community understands and appreciates your genre.
3. **The Group's Culture:**
    - Is it supportive and constructive?
    - Avoid overly negative or toxic environments that hinder your growth.

Reflection Question:
What qualities are most important to you in a writing community? Make a list to help guide your search.

B Alan Bourgeois

Tips for Getting the Most Out of Your Writing Community
Joining a community is just the first step—engaging with it meaningfully is what leads to real growth. Here's how you can make the most of your participation:
1. **Give as Much as You Take:**
    - Offer constructive feedback to others and contribute to discussions.
    - Support fellow writers by sharing their work and celebrating their successes.
2. **Be Open to Feedback:**
    - Accept critiques with an open mind and use them to strengthen your writing.
    - Remember that constructive criticism is meant to help you grow, not discourage you.
3. **Stay Consistent:**
    - Regular participation builds stronger relationships and accountability.
    - Set aside time to engage with your community each week.
4. **Network Strategically:**
    - Build connections that could lead to collaborations or mentorships.
    - Attend virtual meet-ups and interact on social media to expand your circle.

Example:
New writer Lisa started attending monthly critique sessions in her local writing group and quickly built relationships that provided ongoing support and motivation.

Action Step: Commit to engaging with your writing community at least twice a week.

Beyond the Basics

Overcoming Common Fears About Joining a Writing Community
It's normal to feel nervous about sharing your work or engaging with other writers, but stepping out of your comfort zone is essential for growth. Here's how to overcome common fears:
1. **Fear of Criticism:**
   - Understand that feedback is meant to help you, not hurt you.
   - Focus on constructive comments that align with your vision.
2. **Fear of Not Being "Good Enough":**
   - Everyone starts somewhere—communities exist to support growth.
   - View each interaction as an opportunity to learn.
3. **Fear of Commitment:**
   - Start small by attending a single meeting or engaging in one discussion thread.
   - Gradually build your involvement based on your comfort level.

Final Thoughts on Finding a Writing Community
A supportive writing community can be one of the most valuable resources in your writing journey. Whether online or in person, having a group of people who understand your struggles, celebrate your successes, and provide helpful feedback can make all the difference in your career.

Key Takeaways:
- A writing community provides support, accountability, and valuable feedback.
- Explore different types of communities—local groups, online platforms, and conferences—to find what fits your needs.
- Engaging actively and consistently with your writing community leads to growth and meaningful connections.

"The journey of a writer is best traveled with companions."

Action Step: Take the first step today by researching a writing group that aligns with your goals and joining it.

4
Mastering the Art of Editing

Why Editing is Crucial to Writing Success
Writing a book is just the beginning; the real magic happens during the **editing process.** Editing transforms your raw ideas into a polished, engaging story that resonates with readers. A well-edited book stands out, whether you're self-publishing or seeking a traditional deal.

"The only kind of writing is rewriting." — Ernest Hemingway

Many aspiring authors underestimate the importance of editing, but successful writers know that revision is where their work truly comes to life. Editing is not just about fixing grammar—it's about refining story structure, strengthening characters, and enhancing clarity and readability.

What mastering editing can do for you:
- Elevate your writing from good to great.
- Ensure clarity and readability for your audience.
- Improve pacing, tone, and character consistency.
- Increase your chances of getting published or gaining positive reader reviews.

The Different Types of Editing
Editing isn't a one-size-fits-all process. Different types of editing focus on different aspects of your manuscript. Understanding each type helps you identify what your book needs at various stages.

B Alan Bourgeois

1. Developmental Editing (Big Picture Editing)
Developmental editing focuses on the story's **big picture**—plot, pacing, character development, structure, and themes.
Key Areas of Focus:
- Is the plot engaging and well-paced?
- Are the characters believable and dynamic?
- Is the story's structure compelling?
- Does the book deliver on its genre's expectations?

Example:
Imagine writing a mystery novel where the clues are too obvious or the pacing lags in the middle. A developmental editor would help you restructure the plot to keep readers hooked.

Action Step: Outline your book's key plot points and evaluate whether they contribute to a compelling narrative arc.

2. Line Editing (Sentence-Level Polishing)
Once the story structure is solid, line editing focuses on **sentence-level quality**, refining your prose for clarity, style, and consistency.

Key Areas of Focus:
- Are the sentences fluid and easy to read?
- Is the tone consistent throughout?
- Are there redundant words or awkward phrases?
- Does the dialogue sound natural and engaging?

Example:
Instead of writing "She was very angry," a line editor might suggest "She fumed, her hands clenched into fists," to enhance the emotional impact.

Action Step: Take one page of your manuscript and rewrite it with tighter, more concise prose.

Beyond the Basics

3. Copy Editing (Grammar, Style, and Consistency)
Copy editing ensures your writing adheres to grammatical rules, style guidelines, and consistency across the manuscript.
Key Areas of Focus:
- Grammar, punctuation, and spelling corrections.
- Ensuring consistency in character names, timelines, and formatting.
- Adhering to a style guide (e.g., Chicago Manual of Style).

Example:
If your protagonist's eyes are green in chapter 2 and brown in chapter 10, a copy editor will catch this inconsistency.

Action Step: Use tools like Grammarly or ProWritingAid to identify inconsistencies in your manuscript.

4. Proofreading (Final Quality Check)
Proofreading is the final step in the editing process before publication, focusing on **minor errors** and ensuring your manuscript is print-ready.

Key Areas of Focus:
- Catching typos, misspellings, and punctuation errors.
- Checking formatting issues for print and digital versions.
- Ensuring consistent chapter headings, margins, and line spacing.

Example:
A proofreader will catch those sneaky typos that slip through other editing stages, such as "their" instead of "there."

Action Step: Read your manuscript aloud to catch overlooked errors in punctuation or awkward phrasing.

DIY Editing vs. Hiring a Professional Editor

Many writers struggle with the decision of whether to edit their work themselves or hire a professional. While self-editing is a valuable skill, professional editors bring an objective, expert perspective that can take your book to the next level.

Self-Editing

Cost-effective but time-consuming.

Requires deep objectivity, which can be difficult.

Useful for early drafts.

Professional Editing

Offers expert insights and market readiness.

Removes bias and strengthens story weaknesses.

Essential before publishing or querying.

Case Study: Indie author Amanda self-edited her debut novel but later hired a professional editor who helped restructure her pacing issues. As a result, her book received glowing reviews and climbed the Amazon bestseller charts.

Action Step: Set a budget and research professional editors who specialize in your genre.

Practical Self-Editing Techniques

Even if you plan to hire a professional editor, self-editing your manuscript beforehand can save you money and help you submit a stronger draft.

1. Take a Break Before Editing

Stepping away from your manuscript for a few days or weeks allows you to approach it with fresh eyes.

Action Step: After finishing your draft, take at least a one-week break before beginning revisions.

Beyond the Basics

2. Read Your Work Aloud
Reading your manuscript aloud helps identify awkward sentences, overused words, and dialogue that doesn't sound natural.

> **Action Step:** Record yourself reading a chapter and listen for areas that sound unnatural.

3. Use the "Big-Picture to Small-Details" Approach
Edit in layers, starting with the biggest issues (plot, pacing) before moving to line editing and proofreading.

Editing Checklist:
1. Plot consistency and pacing.
2. Character development and dialogue.
3. Sentence clarity and readability.
4. Grammar and spelling errors.

> **Action Step:** Break your revision process into stages and tackle one aspect at a time.

4. Utilize Editing Tools
Several tools can assist with the self-editing process, making it easier to spot errors and improve readability.

Recommended Tools:
- **Grammarly:** For grammar and style checks.
- **ProWritingAid:** For in-depth style, pacing, and readability analysis.
- **Scrivener:** To organize and restructure large manuscripts.

> **Action Step:** Run a chapter through one of these tools and analyze the suggestions for improvement.

B Alan Bourgeois

How to Handle Feedback and Criticism
Receiving feedback from editors or beta readers can be intimidating, but it's an essential part of the editing process.

How to Handle Feedback Positively:
- **Stay open-minded:** Remember that constructive criticism is meant to improve your work, not tear it down.
- **Look for patterns:** If multiple readers highlight the same issue, it's worth revisiting.
- **Don't rush revisions:** Take time to process feedback before making changes.

Case Study:
After receiving feedback that her pacing was too slow, writer Jane revised her opening chapters to start with more action, leading to a higher acceptance rate from literary agents.

Action Step: Ask a trusted beta reader for honest feedback and create a plan to implement their suggestions.

Reflection Questions
1. What part of editing do you struggle with the most?
2. How can you improve your self-editing process?
3. Have you considered working with a professional editor? If not, why?

Final Thoughts on Editing
Editing is where your story truly comes to life. By approaching it with patience, strategy, and an open mind, you can transform your manuscript into a polished, compelling piece of work that captivates readers.

Key Takeaways:
- Editing is an essential part of the writing process—don't rush it.
- Use a structured approach, focusing on big-picture edits first.

Beyond the Basics

- Seek professional help when needed, but start with solid self-editing techniques.

"The difference between a good writer and a great writer is editing."

Action Step: Set a goal for your editing process—whether it's revising one chapter a week or tackling dialogue improvements first.

5
Developing an Effective Marketing Plan

Why Book Marketing is Essential for Success
Writing a book is only half the battle—getting it into the hands of readers is the other half. No matter how compelling your story is, it won't reach its full potential without a solid **marketing plan.** Whether you're self-publishing or traditionally published, marketing plays a crucial role in building visibility, attracting readers, and generating sales.

"Writing a book without promoting it is like waving to someone in a dark room. You know what you're doing, but nobody else does." – Anonymous

An effective book marketing plan helps you:
- **Identify your target audience** and understand their reading habits.
- **Increase book sales** by reaching the right people at the right time.
- **Build your author brand** and establish long-term visibility.
- **Foster reader loyalty** through ongoing engagement and communication.

The Core Elements of a Book Marketing Plan
A successful marketing plan consists of several key components that work together to create a cohesive strategy. These include:
1. **Identifying Your Target Audience** – Knowing who your ideal readers are.

Beyond the Basics

2. **Crafting Your Author Brand** – Establishing a unique presence in your genre.
3. **Leveraging Online and Offline Marketing Channels** – Maximizing exposure through various platforms.
4. **Creating a Pre-Launch and Post-Launch Strategy** – Building momentum before and after your book's release.
5. **Tracking and Adjusting Your Strategy** – Evaluating what works and optimizing accordingly.

Step 1: Identifying Your Target Audience
Understanding who your readers are is the foundation of any successful marketing plan. If you don't know who your book is for, your efforts will lack direction and effectiveness.

Key Questions to Define Your Audience:
- What age group and demographics fit your ideal reader?
- What genres and themes do they enjoy?
- Where do they spend their time online (social media, book blogs, forums)?
- What problems or desires does your book address?

Example:
If you've written a cozy mystery, your target audience may include women aged 35–60 who enjoy light-hearted, small-town settings and amateur sleuths. They might be active on Facebook groups dedicated to cozy mysteries and subscribe to book-related newsletters.

Action Step:
Create a detailed reader profile (age, gender, interests, favorite authors, online habits) to better tailor your marketing efforts.

Step 2: Crafting Your Author Brand
Your author brand is what makes you stand out from the crowd. It's how readers perceive you and your work—your unique

voice, themes, and values. A strong brand helps you build a loyal fan base and gain recognition in your niche.

How to Develop Your Author Brand:
1. **Define Your Unique Selling Proposition (USP):**
    o What makes your books different from others in your genre?
    o Is it your humor, unique world-building, or deep emotional storytelling?
2. **Create a Consistent Visual Identity:**
    o Use consistent colors, fonts, and imagery across your website, social media, and book covers.
    o Consider hiring a designer to create a cohesive visual brand.
3. **Craft a Memorable Author Bio:**
    o Your bio should reflect your writing style and personality.
    o Example: "Jane Doe writes whimsical fantasy adventures with a touch of romance and humor."

Case Study:
Bestselling author Colleen Hoover established her brand by consistently delivering emotional, contemporary romance stories with relatable characters. She leverages social media to reinforce her brand personality.

Action Step:
Write a compelling author bio and tagline that reflects your brand and genre.

Step 3: Leveraging Online and Offline Marketing Channels
Once you've defined your audience and brand, it's time to choose the right marketing channels to reach your readers effectively.

Beyond the Basics

Online Marketing Strategies
1. **Social Media Presence:**
    - Choose platforms where your audience spends time (Instagram for YA, Facebook for cozy mysteries, LinkedIn for business books).
    - Post engaging content such as writing updates, behind-the-scenes looks, and reader interactions.
    - Use relevant hashtags to increase visibility.
2. **Email Marketing:**
    - Build an email list to keep readers updated about your work, special promotions, and new releases.
    - Offer a freebie (e.g., a short story, character guide) to entice readers to subscribe.
    - Use platforms like Mailchimp or ConvertKit to automate email campaigns.
3. **Author Website and Blog:**
    - Your website should include your bio, book list, blog, and contact information.
    - Blog about topics related to your genre (e.g., writing tips, book recommendations, research insights).
4. **Amazon and Book Retailer Optimization:**
    - Use relevant keywords in your book title, subtitle, and description.
    - Encourage reader reviews to improve your book's ranking.
    - Enroll in Amazon KDP Select for promotional opportunities like Kindle Unlimited.

Example:
Self-published author Mark Dawson uses Amazon ads, Facebook ads, and a strong email marketing strategy to generate thousands of sales per month.

B Alan Bourgeois

Offline Marketing Strategies
1. **Bookstore Events and Signings:**
   - Partner with local bookstores to host signings and meet-and-greets.
   - Bring promotional materials like bookmarks and posters.
2. **Speaking Engagements:**
   - Offer to speak at libraries, schools, and writing conferences about your writing journey.
3. **Print Media Exposure:**
   - Submit press releases to local newspapers and magazines.
   - Pitch feature articles to genre-specific publications.
4. **Networking at Industry Events:**
   - Attend book fairs, writing workshops, and literary festivals to connect with potential readers and industry professionals.

Action Step:
Choose one online and one offline marketing strategy to implement in the next month.

Step 4: Pre-Launch and Post-Launch Strategies
Marketing your book doesn't start on release day—it begins months before. A well-planned pre-launch and post-launch strategy ensures a successful debut.

Pre-Launch Activities (3–6 months before release):
- Build anticipation through social media teasers and cover reveals.
- Reach out to book bloggers and influencers for early reviews.
- Set up pre-orders on platforms like Amazon.
- Run giveaways to create buzz and encourage engagement.

Beyond the Basics

Launch Week Activities:
- Host a virtual book launch event (Facebook Live, Instagram Q&A).
- Run promotional ads on social media platforms.
- Offer limited-time discounts or bundle deals.

Post-Launch Activities:
- Continue engaging with your readers via email and social media.
- Pursue additional marketing opportunities such as podcast interviews and guest blog posts.
- Monitor sales data and adjust your marketing strategy based on what's working.

Case Study:
Bestselling author Joanna Penn carefully plans her book launches with strategic content marketing, podcast interviews, and email list promotions, leading to strong initial sales and long-term visibility.

Action Step:
Create a pre-launch timeline with key promotional activities leading up to your book's release.

Step 5: Tracking and Adjusting Your Strategy

Marketing is not a one-time effort—it's an ongoing process that requires analysis and adaptation. Tracking your marketing efforts allows you to see what's working and adjust accordingly.

Tools to Track Marketing Efforts:
- **Google Analytics:** Monitor website traffic.
- **Amazon Author Central:** Track sales and rankings.
- **Social Media Insights:** Measure engagement and reach.

Reflection Question:
What marketing efforts have been most effective in engaging your audience so far?

B Alan Bourgeois

Final Thoughts on Book Marketing

A well-executed marketing plan helps turn your book into a success story. With the right strategies and consistent effort, you can reach your ideal readers and build a thriving writing career.

Key Takeaways:
- Know your audience and tailor your efforts to meet their needs.
- Consistency and persistence are key to successful book marketing.
- Keep testing and adapting your strategies based on performance data.

"Your book is your product; your marketing plan is your launchpad to success."

> **Action Step:** Choose one marketing strategy from this chapter and start implementing it today

6
Building an Online Presence

Why Your Online Presence Matters
In today's digital-first world, an author's online presence is critical for visibility, credibility, and engagement. Whether you're an indie author or traditionally published, a strong online presence helps:
- **Connect directly with readers** and build lasting relationships.
- **Establish your personal brand** and authority in your niche.
- **Sell books more effectively** by driving traffic to sales channels.

"If readers can't find you online, they might not find your books either." – Jane Friedman

Key Elements of an Effective Online Presence
1. **Professional Website (Your Digital Homebase):**
    - Essential pages to include:
        - *Home Page:* Clear branding, featured books, recent news.
        - *About Page:* A compelling author bio with a personal touch.
        - *Books Page:* Summaries, reviews, and purchase links.
        - *Contact Page:* Easy ways for readers to reach you.

    Example: Author Brandon Sanderson updates his website regularly with book progress updates, creating anticipation and engagement with his readers.

B Alan Bourgeois

> **Action Step:** Start with a simple website using platforms like WordPress or Wix.

2. **Social Media (Your Engagement Hub):**
   - Choose platforms that align with your audience:
     - *Instagram:* Visual storytelling, ideal for YA and romance authors.
     - *Twitter (X):* Great for connecting with the writing community.
     - *Facebook:* Ideal for reader groups and book launch events.
     - *TikTok:* Growing space for authors using #BookTok.
   -

   Case Study: Colleen Hoover leveraged Instagram and TikTok to create viral buzz, turning her books into bestsellers.

   Action Step: Post three types of content weekly: personal insights, writing tips, and book-related news.

3. **Email Marketing (Your Direct Connection):**
   - Build an email list to maintain direct contact with readers.
   - Offer a freebie like a short story or sample chapters in exchange for sign-ups.
   - Use platforms like Mailchimp or ConvertKit for automation.

   Example: Joanna Penn sends monthly newsletters with writing updates, offering exclusive sneak peeks to her subscribers.

   Action Step: Set up an email sign-up form on your website today.

Beyond the Basics

Reflection Question
Which platform aligns best with your personality and target audience?

Exercise
Draft a sample social media post that introduces you and your writing style to new readers.

7
Setting Realistic Goals

Why Goal-Setting Matters for Writers
Writing a book is a long-term endeavor, and without clear goals, it's easy to feel overwhelmed or stuck in a cycle of procrastination. Successful writers don't just rely on inspiration; they set **intentional, achievable goals** that guide their creative process.

Effective goal-setting helps you:
- **Stay focused:** Clear goals keep you on track and prevent distractions.
- **Build momentum:** Small wins add up, making large projects feel manageable.
- **Measure progress:** Tangible milestones provide motivation and a sense of achievement.
- **Overcome self-doubt:** Achieving goals helps combat imposter syndrome and builds confidence.

"A goal without a plan is just a wish." – Antoine de Saint-Exupéry

Breaking Down Goals into Manageable Steps
Many writers set vague goals like "I want to finish my book," but without structure, these ambitions often fall by the wayside. The key to success is breaking down larger aspirations into smaller, manageable steps.

> **Example:** Instead of setting a goal to "publish a novel," break it down like this:
> 1. **Month 1:** Develop a detailed outline and character profiles.
> 2. **Month 2-4:** Write 1,000 words a day to complete a first draft.

Beyond the Basics

3. **Month 5:** Revise the manuscript with feedback from beta readers.
4. **Month 6:** Query agents or explore self-publishing options.

This approach makes the process feel less daunting and allows you to celebrate progress along the way.

Using SMART Goals to Stay on Track

A proven method for effective goal-setting is the **SMART framework**, ensuring your goals are:
- **Specific:** Clear and well-defined objectives (e.g., "Write 500 words daily" instead of "Write more").
- **Measurable:** Trackable progress with tangible outcomes (e.g., "Complete 20,000 words in 30 days").
- **Achievable:** Realistic within your current lifestyle and commitments.
- **Relevant:** Aligned with your broader writing aspirations.
- **Time-bound:** Set deadlines to maintain momentum (e.g., "Finish the first draft by September 30th").
-

Example SMART Goal:

"I will write 3,000 words per week for the next two months to complete my first draft by June 1st."

Common Pitfalls Writers Face in Goal-Setting (And How to Avoid Them)

1. **Setting Unrealistic Expectations:**
   - *Pitfall:* Attempting to write 10,000 words a day and burning out.
   - *Solution:* Start with achievable goals and gradually increase output.
2. **Lack of Accountability:**
   - *Pitfall:* Without accountability, it's easy to let goals slip.
   - *Solution:* Join a writing group or find an accountability partner to stay on track.

3. **Failure to Track Progress:**
    - *Pitfall:* Losing motivation due to a lack of visible progress.
    - *Solution:* Use writing trackers, planners, or apps like Trello or Scrivener to log progress.

Examples of Successful Writers Who Set Goals
- **Brandon Sanderson:** Known for setting ambitious, structured goals that allow him to write multiple books a year while maintaining quality.
- **Stephen King:** Writes 2,000 words every day with a clear routine, ensuring a steady output without burnout.
- **Case Study:** Sarah, an aspiring fantasy writer, struggled with completing her novel. By implementing a SMART goal strategy—writing 1,000 words a day and tracking her progress—she completed her first draft within six months.

Practical Goal-Setting Strategies
1. **Create a Writing Schedule:**
    - Establish dedicated writing times each day or week to maintain consistency.
    - Example: "Write every morning from 7–8 AM before work."
2. **Use the Pomodoro Technique:**
    - Write in focused 25-minute sessions with 5-minute breaks to maximize productivity.
    - Tools: Use apps like Focus Booster to track sessions.
3. **Celebrate Small Wins:**
    - Reward yourself when you hit milestones—treat yourself to a coffee or a movie after reaching 10,000 words.
4. **Utilize Writing Challenges:**

Beyond the Basics

- Participate in programs like NaNoWriMo (National Novel Writing Month) to set and achieve ambitious short-term goals.

Tracking Your Progress
Keeping track of your writing goals helps you stay accountable and adjust when needed. Here are a few ways to track progress:
- **Writing Journals:** Log your daily or weekly word counts and reflections.
- **Goal-Tracking Apps:** Use apps like Notion, Evernote, or Google Sheets to monitor progress.
- **Accountability Partners:** Check in with a fellow writer weekly to share progress.

Example Tracking Template:

Date	Goal	Progress	Notes
March 1	Write 1,000 words	1,200 words	Feeling great today!
March 2	Outline Chapter 3	Completed	Found plot hole, fixing.
March 3	Research for Chapter 4	Halfway	Need to revisit sources.

Reflection Questions
- What writing goals have you set in the past, and why did they succeed or fail?
- What obstacles typically prevent you from achieving your goals?
- How can you break your current writing goal into smaller, actionable steps?

Exercises to Put Goal-Setting into Action
1. **Set Your Writing Goal:**
    - Choose a goal for the next 30 days (e.g., "Write 10,000 words by the end of the month").

- Break it into weekly targets.
2. **Create a Progress Chart:**
    - Use a calendar or spreadsheet to log daily progress.
    - Mark milestones and celebrate achievements.
3. **Identify Accountability Partners:**
    - Find a fellow writer or join an online writing group to report weekly progress.

Final Thoughts on Goal-Setting
Setting realistic goals is one of the most powerful tools a writer can use to turn their dreams into reality. The key is to find what works best for your lifestyle and creative process. Whether you're writing your first novel or juggling multiple projects, staying committed to your goals will pave the way for long-term success.

> **Action Step:** Take 10 minutes right now to write down your writing goals for the next 3 months using the SMART method. Keep it somewhere visible to stay focused and motivated.

8
Handling Rejection

Why Rejection is an Inevitable Part of a Writer's Journey
Rejection is a rite of passage for every writer, from aspiring novelists to best-selling authors. Whether it comes from literary agents, publishers, or even readers, rejection can feel discouraging—but it's not the end of the road. Instead, rejection can serve as a tool for growth, helping you refine your craft, build resilience, and ultimately find success.

"I have received rejections—thousands of them—but they made me a better writer." — Stephen King

J.K. Rowling, Stephen King, and Agatha Christie all faced multiple rejections before their books became worldwide phenomena. The difference between writers who succeed and those who give up is how they respond to rejection.

Understanding Why Writers Get Rejected
Receiving a rejection doesn't always mean your writing isn't good enough. There are various reasons why a manuscript might not be accepted, and understanding these reasons can help you adjust your approach and move forward.
Common Reasons for Rejection:
1. **Your Manuscript Isn't the Right Fit:**
    - Agents and publishers have specific tastes and market needs.
    - *Solution:* Research thoroughly before submitting to ensure alignment with their interests.

2. **The Market is Oversaturated:**
   - Some genres or topics might already be overcrowded.
   - *Solution:* Consider unique angles or niche audiences to differentiate your work.
3. **Your Manuscript Needs More Work:**
   - Structural issues, pacing problems, or underdeveloped characters could be barriers.
   - *Solution:* Seek feedback from beta readers or a professional editor.
4. **It's Just Not the Right Time:**
   - Publishing trends shift, and timing plays a crucial role.
   - *Solution:* Stay patient and persistent, resubmitting when the timing is better.

Turning Rejection into Growth

Every "no" can be a step closer to "yes" if you learn how to use rejection as a learning experience. Instead of taking it personally, view rejection as valuable feedback that can propel your writing career forward.

Steps to Handle Rejection Effectively:

1. **Process Your Emotions:**
   - It's natural to feel disappointed, but don't let rejection define your worth.
   - Take a short break, regroup, and refocus.
2. **Seek Constructive Feedback:**
   - If an agent or editor provides feedback, analyze it objectively and identify common themes.
   - Use writing critique groups to get additional perspectives.
3. **Revise and Improve:**
   - Incorporate feedback thoughtfully and objectively without compromising your authentic voice.

Beyond the Basics

- Work through multiple revisions before resubmitting.
4. **Broaden Your Horizons:**
    - If traditional publishing isn't working, consider self-publishing or hybrid publishing models.
    - Submit to literary magazines, contests, or small presses to build credentials.

Example: After receiving numerous rejections, Andy Weir self-published *The Martian* on his blog, which led to a major publishing deal and a movie adaptation.

Strategies to Stay Resilient After Rejection

Building emotional resilience is key to long-term success. Here are some practical ways to stay motivated after facing rejection:

1. **Adopt a Growth Mindset:**
    - View rejection as part of the learning process rather than a personal failure.
    - Remind yourself that every successful author faced rejection before breaking through.
2. **Create a Rejection Ritual:**
    - Have a system in place to process rejections, such as writing them down in a "rejection journal" with lessons learned.
    - Treat yourself to something small, like a favorite treat or activity, to acknowledge your effort.
3. **Surround Yourself with Support:**
    - Join writing groups, both online and offline, to share experiences and gain encouragement.
    - Follow authors who have overcome rejection and learn from their journeys.
4. **Keep Writing:**
    - The best way to overcome rejection is to keep creating new work.
    - Use rejection as fuel to refine your craft and move on to the next project.

Case Study: Margaret Mitchell's *Gone with the Wind* was rejected 38 times before becoming a bestseller. Her persistence ultimately paid off, and the book remains a classic today.

Practical Ways to Track and Manage Submissions

Keeping track of your submissions helps you stay organized and strategic about where and when you submit your work.

Submission Tracking Template Example:

Submission Date	Agent/Publisher	Response Received	Feedback Given	Next Steps
March 1, 2024	Jane Doe Agency	Rejected	Form rejection	Submit to next agent
April 10, 2024	ABC Publishing	Requested full	Needs pacing edits	Revise and resubmit

Use tools like:
- **Google Sheets** to track submissions.
- **Trello or Notion** to organize responses and next steps.
- **Submittable.com** for tracking magazine and contest entries.

Action Step:
Create a submission tracking system today to monitor your queries and follow-ups efficiently.

How to Use Rejection as Motivation

Instead of letting rejection discourage you, turn it into fuel to keep pushing forward. Some productive ways to harness rejection include:
- **Revising with Purpose:** Use rejection feedback as a roadmap for improvement.
- **Finding Inspiration in Setbacks:** Read success stories of authors who overcame rejection.

Beyond the Basics

- **Challenging Yourself:** Set a goal to submit to a certain number of agents or contests within a specific time frame.

Reflection Questions
1. How do you typically respond to rejection, and what can you do differently?
2. What's one positive lesson you've learned from a rejection?
3. How can you use feedback to strengthen your current manuscript?

Exercises to Build Resilience
1. **Rejection Letter Analysis:**
   - Gather past rejection letters and identify common patterns in the feedback.
   - Create an action plan to address recurring issues.
2. **Reframe the Narrative:**
   - Write a letter to yourself reframing rejection as a learning opportunity rather than a failure.
3. **Positive Affirmations Exercise:**
   - List three reasons why you're proud of your writing journey, regardless of rejection.

Final Thoughts on Rejection
Rejection is an unavoidable part of the writing journey, but how you handle it determines your success. By shifting your mindset and continuing to refine your craft, you'll turn each rejection into an opportunity for growth. Remember, every great author faced obstacles—but they persevered, and so can you.

Key Takeaways:
- Rejection is not a reflection of your talent but rather an opportunity to improve and grow.
- Use rejection as a learning tool to refine your work and explore new opportunities.

B Alan Bourgeois

- Stay persistent, resilient, and focused on your long-term goals.

"Failure is simply the opportunity to begin again, this time more intelligently." – Henry Ford

> **Action Step:** Write down three strategies you'll use to stay motivated after your next rejection, and revisit them when needed.

9
Seeking Professional Help

Why Seeking Professional Help Matters
Writing is often seen as a solitary pursuit, but achieving success in today's publishing landscape requires collaboration. Professional help can take your writing from good to great by providing expertise, industry knowledge, and a fresh perspective. Whether you're aiming for traditional publishing or self-publishing, investing in the right professional support can save you time, frustration, and costly mistakes.

"Great writing is rewriting. And great rewriting often needs an outside perspective." – Ernest Hemingway

Many successful authors—whether bestselling or indie—hire professionals at various stages of their careers. Recognizing when you need help and where to find it is a critical skill for a thriving writing career.

Signs You Might Need Professional Assistance
1. **You Feel Stuck in Your Revisions:**
    - If you've edited your manuscript multiple times and still feel unsure, a professional editor can provide clarity.
    - *Example:* After struggling with structure, writer Jane Doe hired a developmental editor who helped her identify pacing issues that she hadn't noticed.
2. **Your Book Isn't Getting Traction:**
    - If your self-published book isn't selling or agents aren't responding to your queries, professional help with marketing or query letters might be the key.

- o *Example:* Self-published author Mike revamped his book description with a marketing consultant and saw a 50% increase in sales.
3. **You're Overwhelmed by the Publishing Process:**
   - o If you feel lost in the complexities of book formatting, marketing, or distribution, professionals can provide much-needed guidance.
   - o *Solution:* Hiring a publishing consultant can walk you through the steps.

Types of Professional Help Available to Writers

Different stages of the writing and publishing journey require different kinds of professional assistance. Here's an overview of the most valuable services available:

1. Editorial Services (For improving your manuscript)
- **Developmental Editing:**
  - o Focuses on big-picture elements such as plot, pacing, and character development.
  - o *Best for:* Writers with a completed draft who need feedback on story structure.
  - o *Cost:* $0.02–$0.10 per word depending on the editor's experience.
- **Copy Editing:**
  - o Improves sentence structure, grammar, and style while maintaining your voice.
  - o *Best for:* Writers preparing for publication.
  - o *Example:* Joanna Penn credits her success to thorough copy editing before self-publishing.
- **Proofreading:**
  - o Focuses on catching minor errors such as typos and formatting inconsistencies.
  - o *Best for:* Final polish before publication.
  - o Tools like Grammarly or ProWritingAid can complement human proofreaders but not replace them.

Beyond the Basics

Action Step:
Research reputable freelance editors on platforms such as Reedsy or Editorial Freelancers Association.

2. Literary Agents (For traditional publishing)
- A literary agent acts as your advocate in the publishing industry, helping you secure a book deal, negotiate contracts, and connect with publishers.
- They are particularly helpful for writers who:
  - Want to pursue traditional publishing.
  - Need help navigating submission guidelines.
  - Seek opportunities for foreign rights or film deals.

Example: J.K. Rowling's literary agent played a key role in securing the Harry Potter publishing deal.

How to Find an Agent:
- Use directories like *QueryTracker* or *Manuscript Wish List.*
- Attend writing conferences and pitch your book in person.

Action Step:
Draft a compelling query letter and start researching agents who specialize in your genre.

3. Book Cover Designers (For self-published authors)
A professional book cover is one of the most critical factors in whether readers pick up your book. A great cover conveys the genre, tone, and professionalism of your book.

Key Elements of a Great Cover Design:
- Eye-catching visuals that align with the genre.
- Clear, readable typography.
- Consistent branding across all formats (eBook, paperback, audiobook).

Case Study: Indie author Amanda Hocking attributed much of her success to investing in high-quality, genre-specific cover designs that stood out in online bookstores.

Where to Find Cover Designers:
- Platforms like 99designs, Reedsy, and Fiverr.
- Genre-specific Facebook groups where designers showcase their work.

Action Step:
Compare book covers in your genre and create a mood board before hiring a designer.

4. Marketing Consultants (For boosting visibility)
Book marketing is essential for sales success, but it can be overwhelming. Marketing professionals can help with:
- **Brand Development:** Positioning you as an author in your niche.
- **Social Media Strategy:** Crafting content that engages readers and grows your audience.
- **Advertising Campaigns:** Running ads on platforms like Amazon, Facebook, and BookBub.

Example: Romance author Penny Reid used a book marketing consultant to craft an Instagram campaign that boosted her visibility and built a strong reader community.

How to Choose the Right Marketing Help:
- Look for consultants with proven experience in your genre.
- Ask for case studies or testimonials before hiring.

Action Step:
Outline a marketing plan and identify areas where professional help could amplify your efforts.

Beyond the Basics

5. Publishing Consultants (For self-publishing guidance)
Self-publishing requires mastering multiple roles—author, publisher, marketer. A publishing consultant can guide you through:
- ISBN and copyright registration.
- Distribution options (Amazon KDP, IngramSpark, etc.).
- Formatting for print and eBook.

Example: Self-published thriller author Mark Dawson hired a consultant to optimize his Amazon ads, leading to a significant revenue increase.

Action Step:
Identify the most confusing aspect of self-publishing for you and seek guidance in that area.

Where to Find Reliable Professionals
Finding trustworthy professionals can feel daunting, but here are some vetted resources:
- **Editorial Freelancers Association (EFA):** A database of experienced editors.
- **Reedsy:** A marketplace for vetted editors, designers, and marketers.
- **Alliance of Independent Authors (ALLi):** Offers directories and vetted service providers.
- **Local Writing Groups & Conferences:** Recommendations from fellow writers.

Tip: Always request samples of work and read reviews before hiring anyone.

Reflection Questions
1. What aspects of your writing process could benefit from professional help?
2. Have you budgeted for professional services, and if not, how can you prioritize?

3. What area (editing, marketing, publishing) do you find most challenging?

Exercises to Take Action
1. **Assess Your Needs:**
   - Make a list of your strengths and weaknesses as a writer.
   - Determine which areas would benefit most from professional assistance.
2. **Budget Planning:**
   - Research the average costs of professional services and create a realistic budget.
3. **Create a Professional Help Action Plan:**
   - Set goals for when and how you'll seek help (e.g., hiring an editor before Q4).

Final Thoughts
Seeking professional help isn't a sign of weakness—it's a strategic step toward achieving your writing goals. Whether you need an editor, a marketing expert, or a publishing consultant, the right support can transform your writing career.

Key Takeaways:
- Know when to seek professional assistance to elevate your writing.
- Invest wisely in services that align with your publishing goals.
- Collaboration is key to taking your book to the next level.

"Success doesn't happen in isolation. Seek help, learn, and grow."

> **Action Step:** Identify one area where you could benefit from professional help and research potential service providers this week.

10
Staying True to Your Authentic Voice

Why Authenticity Matters in Writing
In a world filled with trends, market demands, and social media pressure, it's easy to lose sight of your authentic voice. However, staying true to yourself as a writer is what sets you apart and helps you build a loyal readership. Readers are drawn to stories that feel genuine and resonate with their emotions. Your unique perspective, experiences, and writing style are what make your work truly special.

"To be yourself in a world that is constantly trying to make you something else is the greatest accomplishment." – Ralph Waldo Emerson

Authenticity in writing isn't just about writing what you know—it's about writing what you *feel* and what matters to you. When you embrace your voice, your writing becomes more compelling, engaging, and honest.

What Does It Mean to Have an Authentic Voice?
Your authentic voice is the unique way you express yourself through words. It includes your:
- **Writing Style:** The tone, rhythm, and word choices that naturally flow when you write.
- **Perspective:** Your personal worldview, experiences, and values that shape your storytelling.
- **Emotional Truth:** Writing with honesty and vulnerability, allowing readers to connect deeply with your work.

Example: Haruki Murakami found his authentic voice by blending Western literary influences with his Japanese culture, creating a style that resonated globally while staying true to himself.

Action Step: Take 10 minutes to free-write about a personal experience in your natural voice—without worrying about grammar or style.

Signs You Might Be Losing Your Authentic Voice
It's common for writers to drift away from their authentic voice, often due to external pressures or self-doubt. Here are some signs that you may be losing your voice:
1. **You're Writing to Fit Trends:**
    - If you're forcing your writing to align with popular genres or styles that don't resonate with you, it may feel unnatural.
    - *Solution:* Write the story you *want* to tell, not what you think will sell.
2. **You're Over-Editing Your Work:**
    - Constant revisions and seeking validation from too many sources can dilute your original style.
    - *Solution:* Trust your instincts and embrace imperfections in your writing.
3. **Your Writing Feels Generic:**
    - If your work lacks personality or doesn't evoke emotion, you might be holding back.
    - *Solution:* Infuse your personal experiences and viewpoints to make your writing more distinctive.

Case Study: Author Elizabeth Gilbert struggled with authenticity after the success of *Eat, Pray, Love.* Feeling pressured to meet expectations, she rediscovered her voice by writing what she loved rather than what was expected of her.

Beyond the Basics

How to Discover and Maintain Your Authentic Voice
Finding your authentic voice is an ongoing process that evolves as you grow as a writer. Here are practical ways to nurture and maintain it:

1. **Write from the Heart:**
   - Focus on topics and themes that genuinely excite you.
   - Don't be afraid to tackle subjects that are personal or challenging.
2. **Experiment Without Fear:**
   - Try different genres, perspectives, and styles to see what feels most natural to you.
   - Write short pieces in various tones (humorous, serious, poetic) and see which resonates most.
3. **Read Widely but Thoughtfully:**
   - Read authors who inspire you, but avoid mimicking their style.
   - Keep a journal where you note what elements of their writing appeal to you and how they align with your own voice.
4. **Be Honest with Yourself:**
   - Ask yourself why you're writing a particular story—are you passionate about it, or are you doing it for external validation?
   - Authenticity comes when you write with honesty and emotional depth.
5. **Accept That Your Voice Will Evolve:**
   - Your writing voice will change over time, and that's okay.
   - Embrace the evolution and let it reflect your personal growth.

Exercise: Write a letter to your younger self about why you write and what stories matter most to you.

B Alan Bourgeois

Overcoming Doubt and Fear of Authenticity

Staying authentic isn't always easy—self-doubt and fear of judgment can creep in. Here's how to push through those mental barriers:

1. Stop Comparing Yourself to Others:
- Social media often makes it seem like other writers have it all figured out, but everyone struggles with authenticity.
- Focus on your own journey and progress.

2. Embrace Imperfection:
- Authenticity doesn't mean perfection; it means being real.
- Your quirks and flaws make your writing unique.

3. Find Your Writing Community:
- Surround yourself with fellow writers who encourage you to be yourself.
- Share your work with trusted friends or mentors who support your voice.

Example: Brene Brown, known for her vulnerability-focused writing, built a career by embracing her imperfections and writing openly about her struggles.

How Authenticity Attracts the Right Readers

Readers can sense authenticity—they're drawn to stories that feel honest, relatable, and unique. Staying true to your voice helps you attract an audience that genuinely connects with your work.

Ways Authenticity Builds an Audience:
- **Creates Loyal Readers:** People return to authors who remain genuine in their storytelling.
- **Encourages Word-of-Mouth:** Readers are more likely to recommend books that resonate deeply.
- **Sets You Apart:** In a saturated market, originality is key to standing out.

Beyond the Basics

Case Study: Self-published author Rachel Hollis found success by writing in a relatable, down-to-earth voice that resonated with her audience, leading to best-selling success.

Action Step: Write a short story or blog post in your most natural, unfiltered voice and share it with a small group of readers for feedback.

Reflection Questions
1. What fears do you have about embracing your authentic voice in your writing?
2. Have you ever felt pressured to write in a style that wasn't true to you? What happened?
3. What personal experiences can you draw from to make your writing more authentic?

Exercises to Strengthen Your Authentic Voice
1. **"My Writing Manifesto" Exercise:**
   - Write a list of core values and principles that define your writing.
   - Keep this list as a reminder when self-doubt arises.
2. **Journaling for Authenticity:**
   - Spend 10 minutes each morning journaling in your natural voice without censoring yourself.
3. **Write for Yourself First:**
   - Before thinking about your audience, write something just for you—something you'd never publish. See how your voice emerges naturally.

Final Thoughts on Staying Authentic
Authenticity is the foundation of a successful and fulfilling writing career. By embracing your unique voice, you'll create work that is not only meaningful to you but resonates deeply with readers.

Key Takeaways:
- Your authentic voice is your biggest asset—protect it.

B Alan Bourgeois

- Avoid writing solely for trends or external validation; write what you truly care about.
- Stay true to yourself and trust that your audience will find you.

"There is no greater agony than bearing an untold story inside you." – Maya Angelou

> **Action Step:** Write a personal essay about a defining moment in your life and focus on using your true voice without overthinking style or structure.

11
Time Management for Writers

Why Time Management is Crucial for Writers
Many aspiring and established writers struggle with finding enough time to write amid the demands of work, family, and other responsibilities. Writing requires not just creativity, but also discipline and structured time management to stay productive and meet goals. Without a solid time management strategy, even the most talented writers can fall into procrastination and frustration.

"You don't need more time in your day. You need to decide." — Seth Godin

Mastering time management allows you to:
- Make steady progress toward your writing goals.
- Reduce stress and overwhelm by breaking projects into manageable parts.
- Find balance between writing and other life commitments.

Common Time Management Challenges Writers Face
Before you can improve your writing schedule, it's important to understand the obstacles standing in your way. Some of the most common time management challenges writers encounter include:
1. **Procrastination:**
    - Putting off writing sessions due to self-doubt or distraction.
    - *Solution:* Implement structured writing sessions with specific deadlines.

2. **Lack of Structure:**
    - Writing "whenever I have time" often leads to inconsistency.
    - *Solution:* Establish a consistent writing routine and treat it like an appointment.
3. **Balancing Writing with Other Responsibilities:**
    - Work, family, and social obligations can push writing to the back burner.
    - *Solution:* Prioritize writing without neglecting important life duties.
4. **Perfectionism:**
    - Spending too much time revising and second-guessing leads to lost writing hours.
    - *Solution:* Embrace imperfect first drafts and focus on progress over perfection.

Case Study:
Emma, a part-time writer and full-time teacher, struggled to complete her novel. By setting aside one hour every morning before work and using a weekly planner to track progress, she finished her first draft within six months.

Effective Time Management Strategies for Writers

Below are proven techniques to help you manage your time effectively and stay productive without burnout.

1. Set Clear, Achievable Goals

Without clear goals, it's easy to waste writing time without making progress. Start by setting specific, measurable goals such as:
- "Write 500 words per day for the next 30 days."
- "Finish my novel's first draft in three months."
- "Outline my book by the end of the week."

Action Step:
Write down three short-term writing goals and assign realistic deadlines to them.

2. Establish a Writing Routine
Consistency is key to becoming a productive writer. Identify your most productive hours and schedule dedicated writing time.
Tips for Building a Routine:
- Write at the same time every day (e.g., 6 AM–7 AM or 8 PM–9 PM).
- Link writing to an existing habit (e.g., after your morning coffee).
- Use timers to create structured sessions (Pomodoro Technique).

Example:
Stephen King writes for three hours every morning without fail, treating it as a professional commitment.

Action Step:
Identify your peak productivity hours and commit to writing during that time daily.

3. Use Time-Blocking Techniques
Time blocking is an effective method for organizing your day by setting aside specific chunks of time for different tasks, including writing.

How to Implement Time-Blocking:
- Divide your day into segments (e.g., "9 AM–11 AM: Writing," "2 PM–3 PM: Research").
- Use a planner or digital calendar to allocate time for each writing task.
- Minimize distractions by turning off notifications and setting "Do Not Disturb" hours.

Example Tools: Google Calendar, Notion, and Trello for scheduling writing sessions.

Action Step:
Block out two writing sessions in your calendar for the upcoming week.

4. Prioritize Writing with the Eisenhower Matrix
Not all writing tasks are equally important. The Eisenhower Matrix helps writers prioritize tasks based on urgency and importance.

Quadrants of the Eisenhower Matrix:

Urgent & Important	Not Urgent but Important
Meet submission deadline	Daily writing practice
Revise manuscript for an agent	Research for book ideas

Urgent but Not Important	Not Urgent & Not Important
Responding to social media DMs	Watching random writing videos

Action Step:
Create your own Eisenhower Matrix to identify writing priorities for the week.

5. Break Large Projects into Smaller Tasks
Writing an entire book can feel overwhelming. Breaking it down into smaller, actionable steps makes the process more manageable and less intimidating.

Example Breakdown:
- Step 1: Outline the first 5 chapters.
- Step 2: Write 500 words daily for 30 days.
- Step 3: Revise chapters 1–5 within two weeks.

Action Step:
Take your current project and break it down into at least five smaller steps.

Beyond the Basics

6. Eliminate Distractions and Set Boundaries
Distractions can steal valuable writing time. Whether it's social media, email, or household chores, it's essential to create a distraction-free writing environment.

Tips to Minimize Distractions:
- Write in a quiet space or use noise-canceling headphones.
- Use website blockers like "Freedom" to limit access to social media.
- Let family and friends know your writing time is non-negotiable.

Case Study:
John struggled with constant interruptions but improved his focus by setting boundaries and using the "Forest" app to stay off his phone during writing hours.

Action Step:
Choose one distraction to eliminate during your next writing session.

7. Learn to Say No
Many writers take on too many commitments that leave little time for their craft. Learning to say no to non-essential tasks is key to prioritizing your writing goals.

When to Say No:
- Unnecessary social obligations during prime writing hours.
- Excessive freelance projects that take time from personal writing.
- Volunteering for tasks that don't align with your goals.

Action Step:
Identify one task you can say no to this week to free up more writing time.

B Alan Bourgeois

Reflection Questions
1. What are your biggest time-wasters when it comes to writing?
2. How can you adjust your schedule to prioritize writing without sacrificing other commitments?
3. What small habits can you implement today to increase writing consistency?

Exercises to Take Action
1. **Create Your Ideal Writing Schedule:**
   - Map out your perfect writing day, including dedicated blocks for brainstorming, drafting, and revising.
2. **The 15-Minute Challenge:**
   - Set a timer for 15 minutes and write without stopping. Repeat daily to build consistency.
3. **Accountability Partner Challenge:**
   - Pair up with another writer and share your weekly writing goals for mutual accountability.

Final Thoughts on Time Management for Writers
Mastering your time as a writer isn't about writing for hours every day—it's about making the most of the time you *do* have. With the right strategies, you can build a sustainable writing habit that aligns with your lifestyle and goals.

Key Takeaways:
- Writing success is built on consistency, not just inspiration.
- Time management requires intentionality and discipline.
- Small, consistent efforts lead to big writing accomplishments over time.
-

"Don't wait for the perfect moment. Take the moment and make it perfect."

Beyond the Basics

Action Step: Choose one new time management strategy from this chapter and implement it in your writing routine this week.

12
Self-Publishing vs. Traditional Publishing

Choosing Your Publishing Path

One of the biggest decisions a writer faces after completing a manuscript is whether to pursue **self-publishing** or **traditional publishing.** Each path has its unique advantages and challenges, and the right choice depends on your goals, resources, and personal preferences.

"There is no right or wrong way to publish—only the way that aligns best with your vision."

This chapter will help you navigate the pros and cons of both publishing routes, providing practical insights to help you make an informed decision.

What is Traditional Publishing?

In traditional publishing, an author partners with a publishing house (such as Penguin Random House, HarperCollins, or a small press) that handles:

- **Editing and Formatting:** Professional editors and proofreaders polish your manuscript.
- **Cover Design and Distribution:** The publisher manages book design and distribution to bookstores and online retailers.
- **Marketing and Publicity:** Publishers promote the book through media outreach, author events, and advertising.

Steps in the Traditional Publishing Process:

1. **Querying Agents:** Most large publishers require submissions to come through a literary agent.

2. **Securing a Book Deal:** If an agent takes you on, they pitch your book to publishers.
3. **Editing and Production:** The publisher works with you to refine and prepare the book.
4. **Launch and Promotion:** The publisher leads marketing efforts, but authors are also expected to promote their book.

Pros and Cons of Traditional Publishing

Pros	Cons
Greater credibility and prestige	Lengthy submission and approval process
No upfront costs for editing/design	Lower royalty rates (typically 5–15%)
Distribution to bookstores & libraries	Less creative control over content
Access to professional support	High rejection rates and exclusivity

Case Study:
Debut author Jane secured a traditional deal after querying 50 agents. While it took two years for her book to hit shelves, the publisher's wide distribution network helped her land in major bookstores and literary festivals.

Action Step:
Research at least five literary agents specializing in your genre and study their submission guidelines.

What is Self-Publishing?
Self-publishing allows authors to publish their books independently through platforms such as Amazon Kindle Direct Publishing (KDP), IngramSpark, or Draft2Digital. In this model, the author takes full control of:
- **Writing and Editing:** Hiring freelance editors or editing themselves.

B Alan Bourgeois

- **Cover Design and Formatting:** Working with designers or using DIY tools.
- **Marketing and Sales:** Creating marketing strategies and managing book promotions.

Steps in the Self-Publishing Process:
1. **Prepare the Manuscript:** Hire professional editors and proofreaders.
2. **Cover Design and Formatting:** Ensure the book looks professional across formats (eBook, print, audiobook).
3. **Upload to Platforms:** Publish via Amazon KDP, Apple Books, Kobo, or other retailers.
4. **Marketing and Promotion:** Implement strategies to attract readers through social media, email marketing, and paid ads.

Pros and Cons of Self-Publishing

Pros	Cons
Full creative and financial control	Requires significant upfront investment
Higher royalties (35–70%)	Requires marketing and business skills
Faster time to market	No guaranteed distribution in bookstores
Flexibility in pricing and revisions	Can be overwhelming without expertise

Case Study:
Indie author Mike self-published his sci-fi series and built a following using email marketing and Amazon ads. Within a year, he had sold 20,000 copies and was earning passive income.

Action Step:
Create an outline of your self-publishing budget, considering editing, design, and marketing expenses.

Beyond the Basics

Key Differences Between Self-Publishing and Traditional Publishing

Factor	Traditional Publishing	Self-Publishing
Control	Publisher controls major aspects	Full author control
Timeline	1–2 years to publish	Can publish in a few months
Costs	Publisher covers all costs	Author pays for services
Royalties	Lower (5–15%)	Higher (35–70%)
Marketing	Publisher-led, limited control	Full responsibility
Credibility	High industry prestige	Building credibility yourself

Reflection Question:
What matters more to you—creative control and higher royalties or industry recognition and professional support?

Hybrid Publishing: The Best of Both Worlds?

Hybrid publishing offers a middle ground between traditional and self-publishing. In this model, authors invest in services like editing and marketing while benefiting from professional distribution and credibility. However, authors should be cautious of predatory companies charging high fees without delivering value.

Signs of a Reputable Hybrid Publisher:
- They offer clear, transparent pricing.
- They have proven success stories and testimonials.
- They provide distribution through major retailers.

Examples of Hybrid Publishers:
- She Writes Press
- Greenleaf Book Group

B Alan Bourgeois

Action Step:
Research three reputable hybrid publishers and compare their packages.

How to Decide Which Path is Right for You
Consider the following questions to determine which publishing route aligns best with your goals:
1. **How much creative control do you want?**
   - If you want full control, self-publishing may be the better option.
   - If you're open to feedback and collaboration, traditional publishing could be ideal.
2. **What's your financial situation?**
   - If you have a budget to invest, self-publishing offers a better return.
   - If not, traditional publishing might be a cost-free way to enter the market.
3. **How patient are you?**
   - Traditional publishing takes time but provides validation.
   - Self-publishing allows for immediate results but requires significant effort.

Exercise:
Write down your top three writing goals and assess which publishing model helps you achieve them.

Marketing Expectations in Both Paths
Regardless of which path you choose, authors are expected to play a role in marketing their books. Here's how responsibilities typically differ:

Traditional Publishing:
- Book tours and media coverage organized by the publisher.
- Limited involvement in social media strategies.

Self-Publishing:
- Full responsibility for marketing campaigns.

Beyond the Basics

- Running Facebook, Amazon, and BookBub ads.
- Leveraging book review platforms like Goodreads and NetGalley.

Action Step:
Develop a marketing plan that includes social media, PR outreach, and content creation strategies.

Final Thoughts on Choosing Your Publishing Path
There is no one-size-fits-all approach to publishing. Each route comes with its own rewards and challenges, and the key is to choose the path that aligns with your personal goals and resources.

Key Takeaways:
- Traditional publishing offers prestige, support, and wider distribution but takes time and control away from the author.
- Self-publishing provides complete control and higher royalties but requires significant effort and investment.
- Hybrid publishing combines aspects of both but requires careful evaluation.

"Success in publishing is about finding the right path for you—not following someone else's roadmap."

> **Action Step:** Decide which publishing path resonates with you and create a step-by-step plan to move forward.

13
Monetizing Your Writing Beyond Books

Why Writers Should Explore Multiple Income Streams
While publishing a book is a major milestone, relying solely on book sales for income can be challenging, especially for new or mid-level authors. Diversifying your revenue streams not only provides financial stability but also allows you to leverage your skills and creativity in new ways.

"Don't put all your eggs in one basket—turn your writing skills into multiple sources of income."

By monetizing your writing beyond books, you can:
- Build a sustainable career that isn't dependent on fluctuating book sales.
- Expand your reach and credibility as an expert in your genre or niche.
- Fund future writing projects without financial stress.

Exploring Multiple Income Streams as a Writer
Here are several ways you can monetize your writing skills and build additional income streams:

1. Freelance Writing
Freelance writing allows authors to get paid for their skills while honing their craft. Opportunities range from blog writing and copywriting to ghostwriting and journalism.

Types of Freelance Writing Opportunities:
- **Content Writing:** Writing articles for websites, blogs, and businesses.

Beyond the Basics

- **Ghostwriting:** Writing books, speeches, or articles on behalf of others.
- **Technical Writing:** Creating instructional guides, manuals, and reports.
- **Copywriting:** Crafting persuasive marketing content for brands.

Where to Find Freelance Writing Gigs:
- Platforms like *Upwork, Fiverr, and Freelancer.*
- Job boards such as *ProBlogger, Writers Work, and Contently.*
- Direct pitching to magazines, blogs, and corporate clients.

Case Study:
Sarah, a romance novelist, supplemented her book income by ghostwriting romance novellas for self-published authors on Fiverr. Within a year, she was earning a steady monthly income while working on her own books.

Action Step:
Create a freelance writing profile on Upwork and pitch to at least three potential clients this week.

2. Teaching Writing Through Online Courses

Many writers have valuable insights and experiences to share. Creating an online course allows you to teach writing skills while earning passive income.

Popular Course Topics for Writers:
- How to Write Your First Novel.
- Editing and Self-Publishing Essentials.
- Building an Author Brand Online.
- Writing for Specific Genres (Romance, Thriller, Sci-Fi).

Platforms to Sell Your Courses:
- *Udemy:* A massive marketplace for online learning.
- *Teachable:* Great for building and marketing your own branded course.

- *Skillshare:* A subscription-based platform where students enroll in multiple courses.

Example: Joanna Penn, a successful self-published author, built a lucrative income stream by offering writing and publishing courses on her website.

Action Step:
Outline a basic course structure based on your writing expertise and explore online platforms to host your course.

3. Speaking Engagements and Workshops

Public speaking and conducting workshops allow writers to monetize their knowledge while building credibility and engaging with their audience directly. Many organizations and writing conferences seek experienced authors to teach workshops or give keynote speeches.

Opportunities for Speaking Engagements:
- Writing conferences and festivals.
- Online webinars and panel discussions.
- Schools and community programs focused on literacy.
- Corporate storytelling workshops.

Tips to Get Started:
- Develop a signature talk related to your book's theme or your writing journey.
- Join platforms like *SpeakerHub* to connect with event organizers.
- Offer free webinars to build experience and testimonials.

Case Study:
Author James Patterson frequently speaks at writing events, charging fees while expanding his readership and promoting his books.

Beyond the Basics

Action Step:
Create a short pitch for a workshop idea and reach out to local writing groups or libraries to offer your expertise.

4. Blogging and Affiliate Marketing
Starting a blog allows you to build your brand and generate income through affiliate marketing, ad revenue, and sponsored content.

How Affiliate Marketing Works:
You recommend books, writing tools, or online courses on your blog and earn a commission for every purchase made through your links.

Popular Affiliate Programs for Writers:
- *Amazon Associates* (earn commissions on book sales).
- *Grammarly Affiliate Program* (promote writing tools).
- *Writing-related courses and software (Scrivener, ProWritingAid).*

Example:
Kristen Kieffer, founder of *Well-Storied,* monetized her writing blog through affiliate marketing and digital products, creating a steady income stream.

Action Step:
Choose a niche topic and start a blog offering writing tips, book reviews, or publishing advice.

5. Offering Coaching and Consulting Services
If you have writing or publishing experience, offering one-on-one coaching or consulting services can be a lucrative income source. Many aspiring authors need personalized guidance to overcome challenges and achieve their writing goals.

B Alan Bourgeois

Types of Coaching Services Writers Can Offer:
- Manuscript critiques and feedback.
- Publishing consultation (self-publishing guidance, query letter reviews).
- Author branding and marketing coaching.

Platforms to Promote Coaching Services:
- Your author website and social media.
- Writing forums like *Reddit's Writing Subreddit* and Facebook groups.
- Marketplaces like *Clarity.fm* for consulting.

Case Study:
Indie author Michael La Ronn expanded his income by coaching new authors on self-publishing strategies, generating thousands per month in additional revenue.

Action Step:
Develop a coaching package and offer a free introductory consultation to attract potential clients.

6. Selling Merchandise Related to Your Writing

Authors with a strong fan base can monetize their brand by selling merchandise related to their books or writing themes.

Ideas for Author Merchandise:
- T-shirts, mugs, and tote bags with quotes from your book.
- Signed copies and special editions.
- Writing planners and journals.

Where to Sell:
- Print-on-demand services like *Redbubble, Teespring, and Printify.*
- Directly through your author website using *Etsy* or *Shopify.*

Example:
Fantasy author Sarah J. Maas sells merchandise tied to her

books, further engaging her fan base while earning additional income.

Action Step:
Design one piece of merchandise related to your book and test it with your audience.

Reflection Questions
1. Which monetization strategies align best with your skills and audience?
2. What passive income streams could complement your writing career?
3. How can you balance writing books with these additional opportunities?

Exercises to Take Action
1. **Brainstorm Your Income Streams:**
   - Write down five non-book-related ways you can monetize your writing.
   - Evaluate the skills and resources needed for each.
2. **Set a Financial Goal:**
   - Decide how much extra income you want to generate from writing-related activities in the next 6 months.
3. **Create an Action Plan:**
   - Identify one monetization strategy to start with and break it down into actionable steps.

Final Thoughts on Monetizing Your Writing
Diversifying your writing income isn't just about earning money—it's about creating a fulfilling and sustainable career that allows you to keep doing what you love. Whether you choose freelancing, teaching, or selling products, each income stream builds on your passion for writing while offering financial stability.

B Alan Bourgeois

Key Takeaways:
- Explore different income opportunities that align with your skills.
- Leverage your writing expertise in new ways to attract readers and clients.
- Don't be afraid to experiment with multiple revenue streams to find what works best.

"Success is not about luck, but about designing multiple opportunities."

> **Action Step:** Choose one new monetization strategy and take the first step toward implementing it today.

14
Writing Across Multiple Genres

Why Writing Across Genres Can Be Exciting—and Challenging

Many writers feel drawn to multiple genres, whether it's a love for both fantasy and mystery or an interest in blending romance with historical fiction. Exploring different genres can be creatively fulfilling and expand your audience, but it also presents unique challenges.
Writing across genres allows you to:
- **Expand Your Creativity:** Experiment with different storytelling styles and themes.
- **Reach New Readers:** Attract audiences from multiple markets.
- **Challenge Yourself:** Improve your versatility and writing skills.

However, genre-hopping requires careful planning to maintain consistency in your brand and avoid confusing your readers.

"A writer who writes in different genres is like a chef who cooks with different ingredients—each dish has its unique flavor."

The Pros and Cons of Writing Across Multiple Genres
Before diving into multi-genre writing, it's important to weigh the benefits and potential challenges.

B Alan Bourgeois

Pros of Writing in Multiple Genres:

Benefit	Why It Matters
Increased creative freedom	You won't feel boxed into one type of story.
Greater revenue opportunities	You can tap into different market trends.
Broader audience reach	Gain readers who enjoy different genres.
Fresh storytelling challenges	Keeps writing exciting and prevents burnout.

Cons of Writing in Multiple Genres:

Challenge	How to Overcome It
Audience confusion	Create clear branding and expectations.
Marketing complexities	Separate strategies for each genre.
Maintaining voice consistency	Adapt but don't lose your core style.
Risk of spreading too thin	Plan projects carefully to avoid burnout.

How to Successfully Write Across Genres

If you're considering branching into multiple genres, here are practical steps to do so without sacrificing your brand or reader loyalty.

1. Establish a Strong Foundation in One Genre First

Before expanding into different genres, it's helpful to first establish yourself in one. This allows you to:
- Build a loyal readership that trusts your storytelling.
- Understand the demands of a specific market.
- Develop writing habits and strategies that can transfer across genres.

Beyond the Basics

Example: Stephen King primarily became known for horror but later successfully branched into fantasy (*The Dark Tower*) and crime fiction (*Mr. Mercedes*).

Action Step:
Evaluate your writing career—have you established a solid presence in your primary genre before branching out?

2. Research Genre Expectations and Reader Preferences

Each genre comes with unique storytelling conventions and reader expectations. Jumping into a new genre without understanding its key elements can lead to dissatisfaction among readers.

How to Research a New Genre:
- Read top-selling books in the genre to analyze common tropes.
- Study book covers, blurbs, and reader reviews to understand audience expectations.
- Join genre-specific writing groups and forums.

Example: If you're transitioning from romance to thriller, you'll need to focus more on pacing, tension, and plot twists.

Action Step:
Create a list of three top-selling books in your target genre and analyze their story structure and themes.

3. Adapt Your Writing Style While Maintaining Your Voice

Your writing voice is what makes your stories uniquely yours. While style elements may change based on genre, your core voice should remain consistent to retain reader connection.

Tips to Adapt Without Losing Voice:
- Adjust pacing and language to suit the genre (e.g., faster pacing in thrillers, descriptive language in fantasy).
- Maintain consistent themes or messages across genres.

B Alan Bourgeois

- Use familiar elements (e.g., humor, dialogue style) that readers recognize from your previous works.

Case Study: Nora Roberts successfully writes in both romance and suspense under her own name, but her voice—a blend of emotional depth and strong characters—remains consistent.

Action Step:
Write a short scene in two different genres to see how you can maintain your voice while adjusting style.

4. Consider Using a Pen Name
Some authors choose to write under different pen names when publishing in multiple genres to avoid confusing their audience. A pen name can help differentiate your work and attract the right readers.

When to Consider a Pen Name:
- If your genres are vastly different (e.g., children's books and horror).
- If you want to create distinct marketing strategies for each genre.
- If your existing audience may not follow you into a new genre.

Example: J.K. Rowling writes crime fiction under the pen name Robert Galbraith to separate it from her Harry Potter brand.

Action Step:
Decide whether your multi-genre career would benefit from a pen name or a single author brand.

Beyond the Basics

5. Develop a Tailored Marketing Strategy for Each Genre
Different genres attract different audiences, so your marketing strategies should reflect this. What works for a romance novel may not work for a sci-fi thriller.

Key Marketing Strategies for Multi-Genre Writers:
- Create separate author platforms (websites, social media pages) for each genre.
- Use distinct branding elements such as logos, fonts, and color schemes.
- Cross-promote carefully—introduce one genre to readers of another only if they align.

Example: A fantasy author who starts writing cozy mysteries could promote both on a general website while maintaining separate social media accounts for genre-specific marketing.

Action Step:
Sketch out a basic marketing plan for your new genre, including social media strategies and reader engagement tactics.

6. Build Reader Trust Across Genres
Your readers follow you because they enjoy your storytelling. Regardless of the genre, maintaining authenticity, consistency, and transparency is key.

Ways to Maintain Reader Trust:
- Be upfront about your genre shifts through blog posts or social media.
- Offer free cross-genre samples to introduce new readers to your different works.
- Engage your audience by sharing your reasons for exploring new genres.

B Alan Bourgeois

Case Study: Leigh Bardugo successfully transitioned from young adult fantasy (*The Grisha Trilogy*) to adult fantasy (*Ninth House*), keeping her audience informed and engaged.

Action Step:
Write a social media post or blog entry explaining why you are exploring a new genre and what readers can expect.

Reflection Questions
1. What genres interest you beyond your current writing focus?
2. How can you introduce your existing audience to your new genre?
3. What elements of your writing voice can you carry across multiple genres?

Exercises to Take Action
1. **Genre Blending Experiment:**
   - Write a short story that blends two genres (e.g., a sci-fi romance or a thriller with fantasy elements).
2. **Genre Comparison Chart:**
   - Create a chart comparing your primary genre with the one you want to explore, highlighting similarities and differences in themes, pacing, and audience expectations.
3. **Audience Survey:**
   - Ask your current readers if they'd be interested in exploring different genres with you through a newsletter poll.

Final Thoughts on Writing Across Multiple Genres
Writing across genres can be an exciting way to stretch your creative limits and build a diverse writing portfolio. While it requires thoughtful planning and adaptation, it can also open up new opportunities and creative inspiration.

Beyond the Basics

Key Takeaways:
- Explore new genres while staying true to your core storytelling voice.
- Use pen names strategically if genres are drastically different.
- Manage audience expectations through clear branding and communication.

"Don't be afraid to explore new genres—your next great story might be waiting in uncharted territory."

> **Action Step:** Choose one genre you've always wanted to write in and outline a short story idea to test the waters.

15
Overcoming Writer's Block and Creative Burnout

Why Writer's Block and Burnout Happen
Every writer, from aspiring beginners to seasoned professionals, encounters **writer's block** and **creative burnout** at some point. These obstacles can be frustrating, leading to self-doubt and a loss of momentum. Understanding why they occur is the first step in overcoming them.

Writer's block typically stems from:
- **Perfectionism:** Fear of not writing well enough.
- **Lack of Inspiration:** Feeling disconnected from your story or ideas.
- **Overwhelm:** Trying to tackle too much at once.
- **Self-Doubt:** Worrying about whether your work is good enough.

Creative burnout, on the other hand, occurs when writers push themselves too hard without rest, leading to exhaustion and a loss of passion.

"You can't use up creativity. The more you use, the more you have." – Maya Angelou

The good news? Both writer's block and burnout can be managed and overcome with the right strategies.

The Difference Between Writer's Block and Burnout
Understanding whether you're facing writer's block or burnout is crucial because they require different approaches to overcome.

Beyond the Basics

Writer's Block	Creative Burnout
Temporary difficulty generating ideas	Long-term exhaustion and disinterest
Can be addressed with short-term solutions	Requires deeper rest and lifestyle changes
Often caused by fear or perfectionism	Often caused by overworking or stress
Solutions: Brainstorming, prompts, routines	Solutions: Rest, self-care, gradual return

Action Step: Reflect on your current writing challenges—do they stem from short-term blocks or long-term burnout?

Common Causes of Writer's Block and How to Overcome Them

1. Fear of Imperfection
Many writers freeze up because they feel their writing isn't "good enough." This leads to over-editing while drafting or avoiding writing altogether.
Solutions:
- Embrace the **"shitty first draft"** philosophy (Anne Lamott). Allow yourself to write poorly and revise later.
- Set a timer for 10 minutes and write freely without judgment.
- Remind yourself that every published book started as a rough draft.

Example: Famous authors like Ernest Hemingway and Jodi Picoult admit their first drafts were messy, but persistence led to polished final versions.

Action Step: Commit to writing 200 words a day without editing—just pure creativity.

B Alan Bourgeois

2. Lack of Inspiration
Sometimes the ideas just aren't flowing, leaving you feeling stuck and uninspired.

Solutions:
- Change your writing environment—try writing in a park, café, or a new room.
- Read books outside your genre to spark new ideas.
- Engage in creative activities like sketching or listening to music to trigger fresh thoughts.

Case Study:
Writer Elizabeth Gilbert once overcame a creative rut by traveling and keeping a journal of her experiences, which later inspired her book *Eat, Pray, Love*.

Action Step: Try a 15-minute writing prompt based on an unrelated topic to get your creative juices flowing.

3. Overwhelm from a Large Project
If you're facing an ambitious writing project, it can feel too big to tackle, leading to procrastination.

Solutions:
- Break your project into smaller tasks, such as focusing on one chapter or scene at a time.
- Use the **Pomodoro Technique:** Write for 25 minutes, then take a 5-minute break.
- Outline your work to create a roadmap and lessen uncertainty.

Example: Bestselling author Brandon Sanderson breaks down his massive fantasy novels into smaller daily writing goals to stay on track without overwhelm.

Action Step: Write down three small writing tasks you can tackle today to make progress.

Beyond the Basics

Strategies to Prevent and Overcome Creative Burnout
Creative burnout occurs when writing becomes mentally and emotionally exhausting, often after long periods of pressure or deadlines. Preventing burnout requires a proactive approach to balance writing with self-care.

1. Set Boundaries Around Your Writing Time
Writing should fit into your life in a way that feels sustainable, not forced.

Solutions:
- Set clear boundaries on when and where you write to avoid overworking.
- Prioritize self-care activities like exercise, sleep, and social time.
- Practice saying no to projects that don't align with your long-term goals.

Case Study:
Fantasy author V.E. Schwab schedules specific "off days" where she steps away from writing entirely to prevent burnout.

Action Step: Schedule at least one writing-free day this week to recharge.

2. Reconnect with Your "Why"
Burnout often happens when you lose touch with why you started writing in the first place.

Solutions:
- Reread favorite passages of your own work that made you proud.
- Create a vision board with your writing goals and inspirations.

- Engage with your readers—positive feedback can reignite your passion.

Example: When Neil Gaiman felt burned out, he revisited the stories that first inspired him to write, helping him reconnect with his love for storytelling.

Action Step: Write a short journal entry on why you love writing and what it means to you.

3. Take Intentional Breaks
Stepping away from writing doesn't mean you're giving up; it means you're recharging.

Solutions:
- Take short breaks between writing sessions (go for a walk, meditate).
- Engage in hobbies unrelated to writing to give your brain time to reset.
- Consider taking a longer break if you've been writing intensively for months.

Example: J.R.R. Tolkien took extended breaks between drafts of *The Lord of the Rings,* allowing ideas to develop organically.

Action Step: Plan a short non-writing activity for today that brings you joy.

Practical Exercises to Beat Writer's Block and Burnout
Try these exercises whenever you feel stuck or overwhelmed:
1. **Five-Minute Freewriting:**
    - Write continuously for five minutes about anything that comes to mind—no judgment, no stopping.
2. **Change of Scenery Writing Challenge:**
    - Write in three different locations over the next week and observe how it affects your creativity.

3. **The "What If" Game:**
    - Challenge yourself to brainstorm 10 random "what if" scenarios related to your story. Example: *What if my protagonist had a secret twin?*

Reflection Questions
1. What do you notice about your creative energy throughout the week?
2. What specific triggers cause you to feel stuck or uninspired?
3. How can you integrate small breaks into your writing routine to prevent burnout?

Final Thoughts on Overcoming Writer's Block and Burnout
Writer's block and burnout are inevitable parts of the creative journey, but they don't have to derail your progress. With the right mindset and tools, you can overcome these challenges and reignite your passion for writing.

Key Takeaways:
- Writer's block is temporary; taking action can help you move past it.
- Burnout requires rest and re-evaluating your creative process.
- Small, consistent changes can help you build sustainable writing habits.

"The secret of getting ahead is getting started." – Mark Twain

> **Action Step:** Choose one strategy from this chapter and implement it in your writing routine this week.

16
Writing for a Global Audience

Why Writing for a Global Audience Matters
Thanks to the rise of digital publishing, social media, and e-commerce platforms, writers today have an unprecedented opportunity to reach readers worldwide. Writing for a global audience allows you to expand your readership, increase book sales, and create a lasting impact across cultures and languages.

However, writing for a diverse, international audience requires more than just translating your work—it requires cultural awareness, adaptability, and strategic marketing.

"A great story knows no borders—it resonates with readers from all walks of life."

Key Benefits of Writing for a Global Audience
Expanding your writing beyond your local market can:
- **Increase Your Book's Reach:** Platforms like Amazon Kindle, Kobo, and Apple Books make it easier than ever to sell books internationally.
- **Boost Revenue Streams:** Different regions have varying demand for genres, allowing you to tap into lucrative markets.
- **Diversify Your Readership:** Engaging with readers from different cultures helps you build a more inclusive and widespread audience.
- **Strengthen Your Author Brand:** International visibility enhances your credibility and opens opportunities for

speaking engagements, translations, and film/TV adaptations.

Case Study:
Author Paulo Coelho's novel *The Alchemist* became a worldwide phenomenon after being translated into over 80 languages, proving that powerful storytelling transcends borders.

Challenges of Writing for a Global Audience
While the opportunities are vast, there are several challenges to consider when appealing to an international readership:

Challenge	Solution
Cultural differences	Research and incorporate sensitivity
Language barriers	Hire professional translators
Varying market trends	Tailor marketing strategies by region
Time zone differences	Automate global social media content
Legal and copyright complexities	Learn international copyright laws

Action Step: Research how your genre performs in different regions and identify key markets to target.

How to Make Your Writing Globally Appealing
Whether you're writing fiction or non-fiction, making your book resonate with an international audience requires careful attention to universal themes, cultural nuances, and accessibility.

1. Write with Universal Themes in Mind
Stories that explore **universal human experiences**—such as love, loss, ambition, and family—tend to resonate across

cultures. While cultural specifics add richness, grounding your story in relatable themes helps it transcend borders.

Examples of Universal Themes:
- Triumph over adversity (*The Pursuit of Happyness* by Chris Gardner).
- The quest for identity (*The Namesake* by Jhumpa Lahiri).
- The power of love (*Pride and Prejudice* by Jane Austen).

Action Step: Identify the core universal themes in your book and emphasize them in your marketing materials to appeal to a wider audience.

2. Be Mindful of Cultural Sensitivity
What works in one culture might not resonate—or could even offend—readers in another. Avoid stereotypes, clichés, and assumptions by conducting thorough research and working with sensitivity readers when necessary.

Cultural Sensitivity Tips:
- Use authentic representation by consulting people from different backgrounds.
- Research traditions, customs, and social norms relevant to your story.
- Avoid slang or idioms that may not translate well across languages.

Example: In *Americanah*, Chimamanda Ngozi Adichie authentically portrays Nigerian and American cultures without resorting to stereotypes, making the novel relatable across cultures.

Action Step: Find a cultural consultant or sensitivity reader to review your manuscript.

3. Consider Language Accessibility
Even if you're writing in English, your readers may not be native speakers. Writing in **clear, concise language** with minimal

jargon can make your book more accessible to a broader audience.

Best Practices for Language Simplicity:
- Avoid complex sentence structures.
- Use familiar vocabulary that's easy to translate.
- Provide context for culturally specific references.

Case Study:
The *Harry Potter* series, despite being written in British English, became a global success because of its simple yet engaging storytelling style, making it accessible to all ages and language backgrounds.

Action Step: Run your manuscript through readability tools like Hemingway Editor to simplify language if needed.

Expanding Your Global Reach Through Marketing
Once your book is written with a global audience in mind, you need to market it strategically to different regions. Here's how:

1. Optimize Your Book for International Markets
Different markets respond to different cover designs, titles, and pricing strategies.

Steps to Optimize for Global Appeal:
- Use region-specific book covers and titles where necessary.
- Offer multiple currency options on your website.
- Price competitively based on local purchasing power.
- Offer translations to attract non-English-speaking readers.

Example:
Jojo Moyes' novel *Me Before You* was marketed differently in the UK and US, with distinct covers and marketing campaigns tailored to each audience.

Action Step: Research the top book cover trends in your target regions and adjust accordingly.

2. Leverage International Book Platforms

Publishing your book on multiple platforms increases its visibility worldwide. Consider distributing through:

- **Amazon Kindle Direct Publishing (KDP):** Reach readers in over 175 countries.
- **Kobo Writing Life:** Popular in Europe and Asia.
- **Apple Books:** Strong presence in Western markets.
- **Google Play Books:** Expands your reach into emerging markets.

Case Study:
Indie author Bella Andre published her romance novels across multiple platforms and used region-specific promotions to become an international bestseller.

Action Step: Create accounts on at least two international book platforms and upload your book.

3. Engage with International Readers on Social Media

Social media offers a powerful way to connect with readers across the globe. However, different platforms dominate in different countries:

- **Facebook & Instagram:** Popular worldwide, especially in Western countries.
- **WeChat & Weibo:** Dominant in China.
- **VK (VKontakte):** Popular in Russia and Eastern Europe.
- **WhatsApp Groups:** Growing influence in Latin America and Africa.

Tips for Global Engagement:
- Schedule posts based on different time zones.
- Use hashtags that target specific regions (#BookTokIndia, #AmReadingEurope).
- Share content in multiple languages if possible.

Example:
Author Colleen Hoover uses Instagram Stories and TikTok to engage her international fanbase, often featuring translated versions of her books.

Action Step: Identify the top social media platform in your target country and start engaging with readers there.

Reflection Questions
1. Have you researched how your genre performs in international markets?
2. Are there cultural references in your writing that might need adjustment for a global audience?
3. How can you use social media to expand your reach beyond your current market?

Exercises to Expand Your Global Reach
1. **Cultural Awareness Check:**
    - Choose a key scene from your book and analyze it for cultural references that might need clarification for international readers.
2. **International Marketing Plan:**
    - Draft a simple marketing plan targeting one specific country outside your home market.
3. **Language Test:**
    - Find an online writing buddy from another country and ask them to read a sample of your work for clarity.

Final Thoughts on Writing for a Global Audience
The world is more connected than ever before, offering authors endless opportunities to reach new readers across borders. By embracing cultural diversity, simplifying language, and tailoring marketing strategies, you can successfully expand your readership and make a meaningful impact worldwide.

B Alan Bourgeois

Key Takeaways:
- Universal themes make your writing accessible globally.
- Cultural sensitivity is essential for respectful storytelling.
- Tailoring marketing efforts to different regions increases book visibility and sales.

"A good book can travel anywhere—if you help it find its way."

> **Action Step:** Choose one international market to target and develop a step-by-step plan to reach readers in that region.

17
Leveraging AI and Technology in Writing

Why AI and Technology Matter for Writers
The rise of artificial intelligence (AI) and digital tools has transformed the writing and publishing landscape. From grammar correction and idea generation to book marketing and audience engagement, AI and technology offer valuable support for writers looking to enhance their productivity and creativity. Embracing these tools doesn't mean sacrificing authenticity; instead, they allow writers to:
- Automate tedious tasks, freeing up time for creativity.
- Improve writing efficiency with smart suggestions.
- Reach a wider audience through targeted marketing strategies.
- Stay competitive in an evolving publishing industry.

"Technology will never replace great storytelling, but it can help you tell your story better and reach the right readers faster."

Let's explore how AI and writing technology can complement your creative process and publishing goals.

How AI is Changing the Writing Landscape
AI-powered tools are reshaping how writers brainstorm, draft, and edit their work. Whether you're an aspiring novelist, a freelance writer, or a self-published author, AI can help you streamline your workflow and produce high-quality content faster.

Key Areas Where AI Can Assist Writers:
1. **Idea Generation:** AI can suggest story ideas, plot twists, and character profiles based on writing prompts.

2. **Editing and Proofreading:** Tools analyze grammar, style, and readability to enhance your writing quality.
3. **Marketing and Promotion:** AI-driven insights help writers identify trends, optimize book descriptions, and target the right audience.
4. **Productivity Enhancement:** AI can automate administrative tasks such as social media scheduling and metadata management.

Case Study:
Indie author John used AI-powered book title generators and writing assistants like ChatGPT to help craft engaging titles and improve his book's pacing, resulting in increased reader engagement and sales.

Action Step:
Try using an AI tool to brainstorm ideas for your next writing project and see how it sparks new inspiration.

AI Tools for Writers: Enhancing the Creative Process
While AI won't replace the creative spark that makes your writing unique, it can serve as a valuable assistant. Here are some top AI-powered tools that can help you at different stages of your writing journey:

1. AI-Powered Writing Assistants
These tools can help you generate content, improve clarity, and eliminate writer's block by offering suggestions based on context.

Recommended Tools:
- **ChatGPT:** Provides idea generation, dialogue suggestions, and research assistance.
- **Sudowrite:** AI specifically designed for creative writers, offering plot suggestions and character development prompts.

Beyond the Basics

- **Writesonic:** Helps generate blog posts, book descriptions, and promotional content.

Example Use:
Struggling with dialogue? ChatGPT can help generate authentic character conversations that fit your story's tone.

Action Step: Use an AI writing assistant to brainstorm three alternative endings for your current work-in-progress.

2. AI-Powered Editing and Proofreading Tools
Polishing your manuscript is crucial, and AI tools can catch grammar mistakes, suggest stylistic improvements, and enhance readability.

Recommended Tools:
- **Grammarly:** Checks for grammar, tone, and style issues to enhance writing clarity.
- **ProWritingAid:** Offers in-depth analysis of overused words, pacing issues, and sentence structure.
- **Hemingway Editor:** Highlights complex sentences and passive voice to improve readability.

Case Study:
Fantasy author Amanda used Grammarly to refine her manuscript before sending it to a professional editor, saving time and reducing editing costs.

Action Step: Run a sample chapter through an editing tool and review the suggested improvements.

3. AI-Driven Research and Fact-Checking
AI can help speed up research and fact-checking, ensuring accuracy in your writing while preventing misinformation.

B Alan Bourgeois

Recommended Tools:
- **Perplexity AI:** A research assistant that provides well-cited sources for in-depth research.
- **Quillbot:** Summarizes and paraphrases content while preserving original meaning.
- **Google Scholar (AI-enhanced):** Helps writers find academic sources for non-fiction projects.

Example Use:
Writing a historical novel? AI can quickly provide verified timelines, historical facts, and cultural context.

Action Step: Use an AI research tool to fact-check details in your current manuscript.

4. AI for Marketing and Promotion

Marketing your book is just as important as writing it. AI-driven marketing tools help with audience analysis, ad targeting, and optimizing your promotional content.

Recommended Tools:
- **BookBrush:** Helps design eye-catching book covers and promotional graphics.
- **Publisher Rocket:** Provides keyword and category research to boost book discoverability on Amazon.
- **Canva AI:** Uses smart design suggestions to create marketing materials for social media.
- **ChatGPT for Content Creation:** Generate blog posts, social media captions, and newsletter drafts in minutes.

Case Study:
Self-published author Mark used Publisher Rocket to find niche keywords for his thriller novel, boosting his book's visibility on Amazon Kindle by 40%.

Action Step: Research AI marketing tools to optimize your book's metadata and improve visibility.

Beyond the Basics

5. AI-Powered Audiobook Creation
Audiobooks are a growing market, and AI-driven narration tools allow writers to create affordable audiobooks without expensive recording sessions.

Recommended Tools:
- **Speechify:** Converts text into lifelike narration with different voices and accents.
- **DeepZen:** AI-driven narration with emotional depth and pacing.
- **Amazon Polly:** Converts books into audiobooks with natural-sounding speech.

Example Use:
AI narration tools enable indie authors to create audiobooks on a budget and reach the growing audiobook audience.

Action Step: Convert a short story or excerpt into an AI-narrated audio sample to test audience response.

Ethical Considerations of Using AI in Writing
While AI offers exciting possibilities, it's essential to consider ethical implications, such as:
- **Authenticity:** Ensure that your unique voice isn't overshadowed by AI-generated content.
- **Copyright Issues:** AI tools may pull data from copyrighted sources, so always review content carefully.
- **Overreliance:** Use AI as a tool, not a crutch—your creativity should always lead the process.

Best Practices for Ethical AI Use:
- Always revise AI-generated content to ensure originality.
- Be transparent with your audience if AI-assisted content is used.
- Use AI to enhance, not replace, human creativity.

Action Step: Review your current use of AI tools and ensure they align with ethical writing practices.

Reflection Questions
1. How can AI tools enhance your current writing process without compromising your creative voice?
2. Which AI tools align best with your writing and publishing goals?
3. Are you using technology in a way that complements your workflow rather than complicating it?

Exercises to Leverage AI and Technology in Writing
1. **AI-Assisted Brainstorming Challenge:**
   - Use an AI tool like ChatGPT to brainstorm 10 new book ideas based on your favorite genre.
2. **Editing Comparison Exercise:**
   - Run a chapter through both Grammarly and ProWritingAid, then compare the results.
3. **Marketing Experiment:**
   - Use an AI tool to generate three different versions of a book blurb and test which resonates most with your audience.

Final Thoughts on AI and Writing Technology
Technology and AI tools are here to stay, offering writers new ways to optimize their workflow and reach their audience. While nothing can replace the human heart behind storytelling, these tools can act as valuable partners in bringing your creative vision to life.

Key Takeaways:
- AI can boost productivity, creativity, and marketing effectiveness.
- Ethical use of AI ensures originality and authenticity in your work.
- Balance is key—embrace technology without losing your personal touch.

Beyond the Basics

"The pen is still mightier than the algorithm—use it wisely."

Action Step: Select one AI tool from this chapter and integrate it into your writing process this week.

B Alan Bourgeois

About the Author

B Alan Bourgeois began his writing journey at age 12, crafting screenplays for *Adam-12* as an outlet to develop his style. While he never submitted these works, the experience fueled his passion for storytelling. After following the conventional advice of pursuing a stable career, Bourgeois rediscovered his love for writing in 1989 through a community college class, leading to his first published short story. Since then, he has written over 48 short stories, published more than 10 books, including the award-winning *Extinguishing the Light*, and made his mark in the publishing world.

Recognizing the challenges authors face, Bourgeois founded Creative House Press in the early 2000s, publishing 60 books by other authors in five years and gaining insights into the industry's marketing needs. In 2011, he launched the Texas Authors Association, which grew to include two nonprofits promoting Texas writers and literacy. He also created innovative programs like the Lone Star Festival and short story contests for students, and in 2016, the Authors Marketing Event, offering a groundbreaking Certification program for book marketing expertise.

Despite setbacks during the COVID-19 pandemic, Bourgeois adapted by launching the Authors School of Business, providing essential tools for authors to succeed as "Authorpreneurs." As publishing evolves, he has explored NFTs as a potential revenue stream for writers. With decades of experience, Bourgeois remains a driving force in the literary community, committed to helping authors thrive in a changing industry.

Bourgeois is currently the director of the [Texas Authors Museum & Institute of History](), based in Austin, Texas

Other Books by the Author in this Series

Y'all Write: A Month-Long Guide to Achieving Your Writing Goals

Unlock your creative potential with *Y'all Write: A Month of Writing Celebration and Growth*! This guide offers tips, motivation, and tools to help writers of all levels set goals, build momentum, and embrace the joy of storytelling.

Author's Roadmap to Success: Proven Strategies for Thriving in Publishing

Unlock the secrets to literary success with *Author's Roadmap to Success: Proven Strategies for Thriving in Publishing*. This essential guide provides actionable strategies to help writers build strong habits, master self-publishing, and thrive in their writing careers.

The Writer's Self-Care Guide: Top Ten Steps to Balance and Thrive

Transform your writing journey with *The Writer's Self-Care Guide: Top Ten Steps to Balance and Thrive*. This practical guide offers actionable steps to nurture your creativity, set boundaries, and achieve a balanced, fulfilling writing life.

B Alan Bourgeois

Top Ten Keys for Successful Writing and Productivity

Unlock your writing potential with *Top Ten Keys for Successful Writing and Productivity*. This guide offers actionable strategies to build consistent habits, manage time effectively, and produce high-quality work to elevate your writing

Mastering Research: Top Ten Steps to Research Like a Pro

Elevate your writing with *Mastering Research: Top Ten Steps to Research Like a Pro*. This essential guide provides practical tools and techniques to conduct thorough, credible research and seamlessly integrate it into your work.

Character Chronicles: Crafting Depth and Consistency in Creative Projects

Bring your characters to life with *Character Chronicles: Crafting Depth and Consistency in Creative Projects*. This essential guide reveals professional techniques to develop authentic, complex characters that resonate across any creative medium.

Editing Essentials: Your Guide to Finding the Perfect Editor

Transform your manuscript with *Editing Essentials: Your Guide to Finding the Perfect Editor*. This guide provides practical steps to identify, evaluate, and collaborate with the ideal editor to elevate your writing.

Beyond the Basics

AI Programs Apps Authors Should Use

Revolutionize your writing with *Top Ten AI Programs Authors Should Use*. This guide explores powerful AI tools like Grammarly and Scrivener, offering practical tips to enhance creativity, productivity, and efficiency.

The Business of Writing

Master the publishing world with *Unlocking the Business of Writing*. This essential guide provides expert advice and practical tips to build your author platform, maximize royalties, and turn your passion into a thriving career.

Creating an Effective Book Cover

Create a book cover that captivates readers with *Top Ten Keys to Creating an Effective Book Cover*. This guide offers expert tips and practical advice on design, branding, and marketing to make your book stand out.

Mastering the Art of the Sales Pitch

Master the art of the sales pitch with *Mastering the Art of the Sales Pitch*. This guide provides essential strategies to captivate your audience, highlight your book's value, and drive its success.

B Alan Bourgeois

Publishing Issues Authors Deal With

Overcome publishing challenges with *Publishing Issues Authors Deal With*. This guide offers practical strategies and expert insights to help you navigate rejection, editing, marketing, and more to achieve your publishing dreams.

The Indie Author Advantage: Mastering Control, Royalties, and Reach for Self-Publishing Success

Thrive as an indie author with *The Indie Author Advantage: Mastering Control, Royalties, and Reach for Self-Publishing Success*. This guide offers actionable strategies to retain creative control, maximize royalties, and reach a global audience.

Mastering Amazon Publishing: A Comprehensive Guide to Success for Indie Authors

Achieve self-publishing success with *Mastering Amazon Publishing: A Comprehensive Guide to Success for Indie Authors*. This guide provides proven strategies to navigate KDP, boost visibility, and maximize earnings for your books.

Marketing Essentials for Authors: Proven Strategies to Boost Book Sales

Boost your book sales with *Top Ten Marketing Essentials for Authors: Proven Strategies to Promote Your Book*. This guide combines traditional and digital marketing tactics to help

Beyond the Basics

authors effectively connect with readers and turn their books into bestsellers.

Marketing Mastery: Avoiding Common Mistakes for Authors

Master book marketing with *Marketing Mastery: Avoiding Common Mistakes for Authors*. This guide offers actionable advice to help authors connect with readers, build a strong online presence, and achieve their publishing goals.

The Author Branding Blueprint

Elevate your writing career with *Author Brand Mastery: A Comprehensive Guide to Building and Sustaining Your Unique Identity*. This guide provides practical steps to define your brand, build a professional presence, and connect meaningfully with your audience.

Reader Magnet: Top Strategies for Building an Engaged Reader Community

Build a loyal reader community with *Reader Magnet: Top Strategies for Building an Engaged Reader Community*. This guide offers actionable strategies to connect with readers, create exclusive content, and turn your audience into passionate advocates.

B Alan Bourgeois

Author Platform Mastery: A Comprehensive Guide to Building, Monetizing, and Growing Your Audience

Build your literary empire with *Author Platform Mastery: A Comprehensive Guide to Building, Monetizing, and Growing Your Audience*. This essential guide offers practical strategies to define your brand, engage readers, and expand your reach.

Networking Success for Authors: Essential Strategies Guide

Achieve your literary goals with *Networking Success for Authors: Essential Strategies Guide*. This practical roadmap offers strategies to build meaningful connections, promote your work, and create a supportive community for lasting success.

Write, Publish, Market: The Ultimate Handbook for Author Success
ISBN:

Master the modern publishing landscape with *Write, Publish, Market: The Ultimate Handbook for Author Success*. This guide provides actionable strategies to build your author brand, attract readers, and achieve long-term success in your writing career.

Beyond the Basics

Mastering Interviews: Essential Tips for Authors' Success

Excel in interviews with *Mastering Interviews: Essential Tips for Authors' Success*. This guide offers practical advice to confidently promote your work, connect with audiences, and turn every interview into a memorable success.

Mastering Event Presentations: Avoiding Common Author Mistakes

Captivate your audience with *Mastering Event Presentations: Avoiding Common Author Mistakes*. This guide offers practical strategies to avoid pitfalls, engage your audience, and deliver impactful presentations that boost your confidence and connect with readers.

Survival Strategies for Indie Authors: Overcoming Challenges and Achieving Success

Thrive as an indie author with *Survival Strategies for Indie Authors: Overcoming Challenges and Achieving Success*. This guide provides practical advice and actionable tips to overcome obstacles, enhance your skills, and achieve your publishing goals.

B Alan Bourgeois

Empowering Authors: Top Ten Strategies for Writing Success and Career Growth

Achieve your writing dreams with *Empowering Authors: Top Ten Strategies for Writing Success and Career Growth*. This guide offers practical advice and proven strategies to build habits, refine your craft, and grow your author career with confidence.

The Sacred Connection

Infuse your writing with mindfulness and purpose through *Creating with Spirit: The Sacred Art of Writing and Publishing*. This guide transforms your creative journey into a spiritual practice, empowering you to inspire readers and overcome challenges with authenticity and intention.

Beyond the Basics: Advanced Strategies for Indie Author Success
ISBN:

Elevate your indie publishing career with *Beyond the Basics: Advanced Strategies for Indie Author Success*. This guide offers actionable tips and strategies to diversify income, engage readers, and build a sustainable, thriving career.

Beyond the Basics

The AI Author: Embracing the Future of Fiction

Embrace the future of storytelling with *The AI Author: Balancing Efficiency and Creativity in Fiction Writing*. This guide helps authors harness AI to boost productivity and creativity while preserving the emotional depth and artistry of creating.

The Non-Fiction Nexus: Balancing AI and Human Insight in the Future of Writing

Elevate your non-fiction writing with *The Non-Fiction Nexus: Balancing AI and Human Insight in the Future of Writing*. This guide shows how to harness AI's efficiency while preserving the creativity and ethical judgment that make your work truly impactful.

Authorship Reimagined: NFTs and Blockchain Essentials
ISBN:

Embrace the future of publishing with *NFT and Blockchain Essentials for Authors' Success*. This guide explains how blockchain and NFTs can protect your work, automate royalties, and expand your audience while maximizing revenue.

B Alan Bourgeois

Adapting Success: Your Book's Journey to Film

Turn your book into a cinematic sensation with *From Page to Screen: A Step-by-Step Guide to Adapting Your Book into a Blockbuster Film*. This guide provides practical advice and industry insights to help you navigate the adaptation process and bring your story to life on the big screen.

Beyond the Basics: Advanced Strategies for Indie Author Success

Elevate your indie publishing career with this ultimate guide to mastering advanced strategies in writing, marketing, and global distribution. Packed with actionable tips and real-world examples, it empowers authors to balance creativity with entrepreneurship and build sustainable, thriving careers.

2026: The Ultimate Year for Indie Authors

Make 2026 your breakthrough year with *The Ultimate Year for Indie Authors*. This guide offers practical strategies to optimize publishing, leverage social media, and achieve unparalleled success in your indie author journey.